Copyright © 2023 Lora Condon

All rights reserved

The characters and events portrayed in this book are fictitious. Any similarity to real persons, living or dead, is coincidental and not intended by the author.

No part of this book may be reproduced, or stored in a retrieval system, or transmitted in any form or by any means, electronic, mechanical, photocopying, recording, or otherwise, without express written permission of the publisher.

ISBN-9798399103907

Printed in the United States of America

What To Know Before Reading This Book

Send me your receipt of purchase to get the bonus content! You'll receive the tour guide for the mentioned locations along with the soundtrack to the book with all the links for the videos.

Much of the historical part of this book is true (including some towns, stores, restaurants, and music). Many of the people, conversations, and relationships are not true. Please don't confuse reality with a fictional book.

My love for Italy is told through a beautiful romance inspired by the Amalfi Coast.

If you've yet to visit the Amalfi Coast, don't be a *stunad* [stupid]. Buy a ticket, drink the wine, eat the carbs, and you'll still lose weight.

Bring an extra suitcase for all the wine, limoncello, spaghetti and art you'll buy.

Use this book as your tour guide when you go to Italy! I did all the hard work for you. Go to my website, www.thebeautybuster.com, email me your book purchase receipt and I will email you the complete list of restaurants, hotels, sites and songs listed in the book, plus a little video from me to you!

For a virtual experience, listen to the songs as you get to them in that part of the book and check out the links of the sites along the way.

Also, please join me on one of my International Love on the Amalfi Coast tours.

Follow on:

Instagram: Love on the Amalfi Coast

Facebook: International Love on the Amalfi Coast

Twitter: Thebeautybuster

Get on my email list to get the most up-to-date information, trips and sales. www.thebeautybuster.com

I have to thank my family and friends in America who helped me get to Italy more than once. Much appreciation to those in America and Italy that researched our family history in Postiglione.

It was the greatest gift I ever received. It changed my life for the better and keeps making it better every day. There are not enough words to say, *grazie mille* [thanks a million].

I wrote most of this book during the 2020 Coronavirus quarantine and riots in New Jersey and around the country. I had a lot of time to write, with no excuses, not even fear and worry.

This book is my love letter to Italy. It is also my thank-you letter to God, who gave me the strength to focus on love and beauty amid death and extreme ugliness. I had a lot of time to talk to God, Jesus, the blessed Mother and my spiritual father, Padre Pio. These three laughed at my earthly shortsightedness, put their arms around me and repeated Padre Pio's words....

"Pray, hope and don't worry." - Padre Pio

Research about Padre Pio and you can see live videos of him. He was a REAL guy, which makes his story even more amazing, believable and mystical. Visit his hospital and legacy in San Giovanni Rotondo, Italy. There is a reason over 6 million people a year visit this small town in the mountains.

Put on some opera, get a bottle of wine and enjoy La Dolce Vita.

Tutti si divertono!!

[everyone enjoy]

Lora Condon

Help with editing from: My sister and my mother. They're not book editors, but they're smarter than I am with this kind of stuff. I'm so grateful they're willing to spend their free time helping. The rest of the editing was done with ProWritingAid which I loved. All the remaining mistakes are their fault! Ok, all the mistakes are my fault! They recommended some changes but sometimes the most perfect grammar does not exude the emotion well enough. Even when some things were highlighted by ProWritingAid, my brain just went over it. Apparently, I'm a passive verb offender. I still don't understand what that means. I also don't believe we need a comma before and or but, but that's a thing now as well. I did my best with the resources I had at the time. Editors are expensive and I understand why but I just could not afford one at this time.

Cover art by:

Tristan Thompson   https://www.instagram.com/tristarr.art/?hl=en

Graphic design, formatting the book for print and general support by: Facets of Hospitality - https://www.facetsofhospitality.com/

Publicist and overall cheerleader Helen Myers of 3DotsPR- https://www.3dotspr.com/

Copyright 2023- Library of Congress

Contents

Copyright	
I Dreamed a Dream	2
You've Got Mail	4
I Know a Guy Who Knows a Guy	8
God's Gift	14
My First Summer in Italy	17
Volare	21
Lemon Heavon	26
Cuori Infiniti	29
A Day With Lorenzo	44
We Speak No Americano	52
Funiculi, Funicula	55
San Pietro Hotel	58
Mi Dispiace	64
I Need You Tonight	84
Quando, Quando, Quando	95
Blessed Virgin of the Rosary	99
Back to America	104
2nd Summer on The Amalfi Coast	107
Postiglione	118

Rethinking My Life Plan	124
Il Postino	134
Return To Italy	138
Torna a Surriento - Return to Sorrento	140
Ti Voglio Bene - I Love You	146
Memory Lane	156
Ma La Notte, No or Maybe, Yes	164
Music Box History	172
Lemon Mare	181
Fried Fanuke	185
Little Pink Lights	197
Uncle Funzie	206
Caruso	211
Relief of The Suffering	218
Our Lady of the Rosary	230
La Fine - The End	232

INTERNATIONAL LOVE ON THE AMALFI COAST

From Pavarotti to Padre Pio

Part 1

I Dreamed a Dream

"Midway upon the journey of our life, I found myself within a forest dark, for the straightforward pathway had been lost." DANTE.

What an incredible dream! It was so real. When I awoke, I was not sure where I was and what was happening. Was I really back in heavenly Italy with Lorenzo, or still in the nightmare of being in New Jersey? For a few minutes, I straddled between both worlds.

As I lie there in my bed, I could still feel my lover Lorenzo from 10 years ago; holding me and kissing me. The faint smell of his customized European cologne made me feel drunk with love, and alive with memories. The dream was so real.

All I could think was how did I ever let him go and would he even remember me? How could he forget me? He was my first love, although I'm pretty sure I was not his, but I was his American or *L'americana*. There's no way he could forget me, I convinced myself. Maybe I was just one of his many and the joke has been on me all these years. Maybe he and his friends are still laughing about me, *L'americana*.

Many thoughts and questions came rushing through my mind. Why did we stop writing to each other and where is he now? The last time I saw him was approximately 10 years ago. I'm not sure how Lorenzo and I stopped talking or writing to each other, but somewhere and somehow, it stopped. The last years went by so quickly.

Yes, I'm still single. I can't imagine he's still single considering he's from southern Italy. As far as I know, everyone in Italy gets married, has kids and stays married. They're still so traditional and God bless it. Americans can learn something from staying together and riding life out instead of giving up.

As I became more awake, I obsessed over my dream. I had to find out if he was happily married with kids and achieved his goal of becoming an architect.

Off to the internet I went, to see if I could find him. I had tried searching for him on the internet before over the last few years to no avail. After a while, I stopped searching. It was like trying to find a needle in a haystack, or rather one white grape in a vineyard of red grapes!

My dream of him was so real. I was still lost in his emerald eyes with flecks of Italian sky blue. I had to find him again. Now I am on a mission and before I even finished my first cup of my favorite Scout and Cellar, clean-crafted coffee, I found him online! I was so nervous and excited to click on the link connecting me to him and creating a direct line to these last and lost 10 years.

You've Got Mail

"Eros Ramazzotti has a song where he talks about someone crossing over into infinity and that is where he will see that person again. I have so many people I can't wait to see." Lora Condon

How do I even start this message? What do I say? "Hey, do you remember me from 10 years ago? That crazy American you had summer affairs with?" "Wanna Netflix and chill?" Would he even remember quoting Dante together on our dates? "Tanto gentile e tanto onesta pare" [So kind and so honest, it seems]. After going back and forth in my mind a few hundred times, I kept the first contact simple.

Ciao [Hello] Lorenzo,

It's Mariella from America. Remember me? Can you believe it has been almost 10 years since we last saw each other? I hope you are doing well. Let me know if you receive this message.

Ciao, Mariella.

Before I hit send, I looked up at a little statue I had of Mother Mary on my desk and held it in my hand and asked for her to bless this email. "Have mercy on a single girl and protect my precious heart. Protect me and make a miracle, amen." I prayed.

Not even five minutes later, I heard a ping coming from my laptop. Boom, and there it was; a response from Lorenzo.

The adrenaline started pumping through my veins, my heart

was pounding and suddenly, I couldn't swallow. My hands were shaking and I couldn't decide if I wanted to open it or remain in the dream. I was so afraid that the dream and fantasy would crash and burn.

The last thing I wanted to hear was that he was happily married to the love of his life and he's designing a new and improved wing on the Vatican! It's so selfish of me. If I really loved him, I would want him to be happy. Yes, of course, I want him to be happy.

I want to be happy too! After catching my breath for a few seconds that felt like forever, I clicked on his email and read his response. It looked short at first glance. My heart sank a little. It read:

Ciao Mariella,

It's nice to hear from you. It has been many years. Life is good. Do you come to Italy?

Lorenzo

What? Are you kidding me? That's his entire response after 10 years? What the heck is that supposed to mean? Is he only being polite? Is this his way of saying, "Hi, now leave me alone, you crazy American?" Now, I'm pissed. Can it be any more anti-climatic? Friggen men, I swear. Wow, do I even respond to such lameness? Well, at least he asked a question, so I have to respond. I mean, it's only polite.

Why didn't he mention his wife or kids, or maybe he doesn't have either? I'm more confused now! He must think I'm nuts for reaching out, and now he knows I've been stalking him. God, I'm so embarrassed. Ok, I have to respond and stop being so dramatic. Here I go:

Ciao Lorenzo,

I have not been to Italy in 10 years. I miss it so much and have not had a good meal since. Have you ever been to America? Are you an architect now?

Hungry,

Mariella

Again, I waited for his response. Was this really happening?

Mari,

No, I have not visited to America. No worry yourself, I eat all the good fish, pasta and wine for you. Yes, I am architect. I make ugly things beautiful for the world to enjoy. No one likes ugly. Do you write still?

Totally stuffed,

Enzo

Reading his emails, I found myself with the biggest grin on my face; eating up every carb and calorie free word. I must have read his words ten times to see if I missed any hint of him still having feelings for me or any sign of marriage.

It was hard to face the fact that I found no speck of him wanting me or wanting to see me or missing me after all these years. I'm sure I'm living and reliving this fantasy all by myself, in my euphoric, romanticized state.

Maybe I missed something in translation, but it seems like his English is better. I carefully responded.

Enzo,

Save me some pizza, vongole and red wine. I am coming to Italy soon for work. I have to write a story. Save me a slice.

Totally starving,

Mariella

What did I just do? I got so excited and wrote exactly what I was feeling. I actually have NO plans to go to Italy and I have NO story to write that would require me going to Italy.

Wow, I'm so desperate. I faked a story to get a response from him. Now I'm freaking out because what if he wants to see me? Worse yet, what if he doesn't? As I'm freaking out and going over every plausible scenario in my mind, a half hour passes and he hasn't responded.

He's only 6 hours ahead; so he didn't fall asleep, since I'm only waking up. Now I'm consumed by thinking, what the heck can I write about in Italy and who can I get to fund this trip?

Freelance writing has its perks, but a funded trip to Italy isn't usually one of them. What the heck was I thinking?

Ping! Mail. Please be Enzo. It is.

Mariella,

When do you come to Italy? The pizza is getting cold and the bottle of wine is almost empty.

Enzo

I Know a Guy Who Knows a Guy

"Friendship is everything. It is almost the equal of family." Don Vito Corleone

Ok, that's more like it now. I'm bursting with excitement and my mind is going faster than a Vespa on the Amalfi drive free of traffic. I can't take it. Time to pitch stories to anyone and everyone to get my butt to Italy. What excuse can I make up?

OMG, I need to starve myself in order to fit into any decent bathing suit. Immediately I started praying to the famous priest and mystic Padre Pio, to intercede for me and to make a chubby girl miracle happen.

Then I prayed to mother Mary to have mercy on a single girl and to intercede for me as well. I didn't want to bother Jesus with romance and matters of the heart yet. I felt like a young girl all over again.

Oh yeah, I'm pulling out the big guns for this trip to happen. Who doesn't love, love? After praying, I called the next best, most powerful person I know, my mother.

"Maaa"!!! I yelled this through the phone the way only a Jersey Italian girl can call for her mother. This distinct yell lets a mother know her daughter's next words are going to be very important. I either have great news, a big surprise, or super juicy gossip. It's the kind of "Maa" that actually makes an Italian mother shut-up and listen. That's a big deal.

My parents were basically Marisa Tomei and Joe Pesci from the movie, My Cousin Vinny. Same voices, same passionate or aggressive interactions depending on the way you look at it. The love was deep.

Many people used to even call them Vinny and Mona Lisa. I'm surprised they didn't name me Mona Lisa. I think they were trying to be classy with Mariella.

"Ma, I need a story to write about Italy. I need a topic a magazine or a news organization will actually pay me to go to Italy to write. What can I write about?"

"Waaaaat? Waa haapp-en? When ya goin ta It-ly? What kinda story ya wanna do?"

I don't know why, but my mother and her mother always pronounced Italy: It-ly. Only two syllables, not three. I never had the heart to correct them and I do not know where this came from, but I'm assuming it's a part of the Neapolitan dialect my great-grandfather might have spoken. Maybe I'll find out when I get back to It-ly!

"That's what I'm asking Ma. I need ideas for a good story where I have to go to Italy in order to write it."

"Why ya so *pazza* [crazy]? You sound like you haf-ta go tomorra!"

I heard my father in the background yelling, "*Maddona mia* [my Lady] what she do now? These yutes [youths], ehh."

I could actually hear the air moving behind my ear as I visualized his thumb and two first fingers, squeezed together as he motioned back and forth in the air behind my mother.

While debating on dropping the big bomb, I said, "Ma, I talked to Lorenzo today."

There was distinct silence on the other end of the line. Silence on the phone with my mother means there might as well be horns blaring with red emergency lights blinking and a loud voice yelling, "Danger, danger, watch out."

"Ma… ya there?" I looked at my cell phone to make sure I didn't lose the connection.

Slowly and quietly she said, "*Madonna mia*. Ohhhh, Lorenzo. Is he married? Kids?" Her voice got louder and louder with every question. "Wife? Divorced? Rich? Still in It-ly?"

"Yes, he's still in Italy, but I don't know the rest of the answers."

"Than what the heck did you tawk about? Oh, Jesus, please, you're givin' me *agida* (acid reflex due to aggravation). Those are the most important questions. Stunad! [stupid]. Didn't I raise you betta?"

"You betta find out cause your biological clock is ticking like this and the way you're going, you ain't never getting married," my father said as he stomped his foot channeling his inner Joe Pesci.

"Ma-a-a, (stretched out to 3 musical syllables, each almost becoming its own word). We briefly emailed, and I didn't want to act like I'm stawkin' him. I'll find out when I get there; if I even get there."

"But you were stawkin' him, so now you have to go. I want grandkids already. You're going.

Write about anything, who cares, it's It-ly. Write about pizza, *mutzarel* [mozzarella], wine. I don't know. Write about anything From Pavarotti to Padre Pio. Does it even matta?"

"Well, it only matters how I can get someone to pay for the trip. So it has to be a compelling story I can only write in Italy that some magazine or organization would want me to write. Ma, I really wanna go back to Italy. I need this. I want this. Do you know anyone that can help me?" The Mary statue catches my eye again.

"Ok, lemme think."

A few more seconds of silence that felt like an eternity. I hear her making sounds like she is talking to herself, but then I realize she's praying to Jesus.

She went right to the top. She must want grandchildren badly. I think she and my father did a mini rosary for emergencies and then she came back with an answer.

"Ok, you're gonna call my cousin Luigi. He knows a guy, who knows a guy, who works with some Italian-American Association. Tell him you're writin' a story titled, From Pavarotti to Padre Pio, and ya need to go to It-ly for the truth and to get details you can't get from the *googootz* [squash]."

"It's Google, ma."

"Whateva. Write about opera singers every Italian-American should know and what the songs are about. I don't know how Padre Pio fits into the story, but you bet your bocce balls, no one can say, 'No' to San Pio, so they will say, "Yes", and send you there."

"Wow ma, that's a great idea and you make it sound so easy. Yeah right, they're gonna put my butt on a plane to Italy cause I asked them?"

"Mariella, *sta zeet* [shut up], listen to your mutha for once, please! God will find a way if it is meant to be. *Che sara' sara* [what will be, will be]." I'll start a rosary novena today with my rosary prayer group at church. I'm the only one with no grandkids. Oh Lord Jesus, consider it done. Done! You start a novena for this tonight, young lady, ya hear me; tonight! Not for nutin', Mariella, but it's not like any guys around here are knocking down your door."

"Fine ma, gimme Luigi's numba."

After she gave me her cousin Luigi's number, I called and told him all about our idea for the article titled, *From Pavarotti to Padre Pio–The Stories Behind the Songs*. He loved it and told me he'd make a call to a guy who knows a guy.

So now, I'm officially one guy closer! About 10 minutes later, I received a call from a guy named Tony from one of the Italian-American Associations. I told him my plan, and he agreed as if he was already waiting for me to call and ask him.

Even though it was still morning, I had to have a mini celebration with a shot of my favorite drink of Frangelico.

I put some in my coffee and, of course, I had a little shot for myself. I've always loved the bottle, which is shaped like a Franciscan monk in a brown robe, tied with a white rope just like Padre Pio. The hazelnut liqueur is legendary. Every Italian-American home has a bottle of this and we traditionally save it for Christmas and Easter or special feast days. Sometimes they brought it out to impress the rich Americans because it somehow made us look classy.

We gave them something they had never had before. Think of the drink as a pure, hazelnut, alcohol-based Nutella blended with cocoa, vanilla and coffee. It's so smooth and I looked forward to having more with ice cream later in the day.

That night, I went to my parent's house to celebrate and to find out what my mother wanted me to bring back from It-ly and to alsohear what my mother thought I should do with Lorenzo. This was a serious talk so a serious wine was required. We opened up a bottle my mother was saving for such a time as this. She always hid a special bottle of wine to celebrate. She brought out a bottle of Bookbinder Cabernet Magnum from Scout and Cellar.

This was serious. This wine is as good as you're going to get outside of Italy. I knew she was not only proud of me but hopeful for my potential with Lorenzo. That bottle went down so fast between the three of us because it is so smooth like velvet.

I gave my mom a sad look when it was gone and she gave me a wink and went underneath the kitchen sink and pulled out another bottle of Bookbinder Magnum. My father was shocked.

She looked at him and said, "Not like you're ever gonna go under the sink and grab any cleaning supplies."

We all laughed so hard and I told my mother she now needs to find a new hiding place.

Two weeks later and a few emails to Lorenzo and I was on the plane to It-ly. The best part of being Italian is when your mother wants something, she will get it, especially if it involves getting grandchildren.

There is also nothing better than knowing a guy who knows a guy! That's what makes the Italian world go round.

God's Gift

"The Amalfi Coast is the terrace of infinity."
FABRIZIO CARAMAGNA

The Amalfi Coast is God's gift to the world. I'm guessing when God was creating the world, he thought to himself, "Hmm... what can I create that fully encompasses all the best things I've ever created and put them in one spot?" His answer to himself was the Amalfi Coast!

The beauty brings tears to your eyes. You can't even believe what your eyes are seeing. It's a living Technicolor postcard. Italy goes to your soul and reminds you that life is short, so appreciate every beautiful moment and squeeze the most out of every second.

Slow food is the rage around the world, but it's really the way Italy has been cooking and living forever. I'm probably biased, but I'm pretty convinced the Amalfi Coast of Italy has the best food, scenery, weather, wine, shopping, landscape, and, of course, some of the most beautiful people.

The men. Ok, we can stop right there. The men are gorgeous and they know it and it's totally ok because why deny the truth?

No need to pretend they're not sexy as anything and ready and waiting to please every woman that exists. Yes, and thank-you, I do deserve to be pleased by a sexy Italian man!

OMG, I almost forgot about the gelato! I'll do just about anything for a gelato. I know I'm not the only one who dreams and desires these creamy, sweet scoops of love.

Part 2

My First Summer in Italy

"Here begins a new life." Dante Alighieri

Finally, the first peace and quiet I'm getting is on the plane. During everything that happened the last two weeks, I never got the chance to sit down and reminisce about the two incredible summers I spent in Italy. Now, I can sit and absorb the magnitude of the last 10 years and how excited I am to be traveling back to this spectacular country.

It all started when my family let me go to Italy for the summer with their best friends, the Volpes, along with their daughters, who were a little older than myself. The Volpes spent most of their summers on the Amalfi Coast and were always talking about how they couldn't wait to go back.

I was absolutely shocked my parents let me leave and get out from under their wings; which were actually armed with wooden spoons so they could hit me from any direction, like an octopus.

When you have Italian parents, you're never too old to get hit with a wooden spoon, shoe or back of the hand. Till the day your parents die, you're young enough to get hit if you step out of line. Trust me. I even got a wooden spoon with my name painted on it for my birthday one year! Thanks Grandma!

On the plane trip to Italy, Mr. Volpe sat next to me and told me the four rules of going to Italy with his family. As my guardian, he was feeling extra protective.

I also knew as my Italian guardian, he had the right to hit me like my parents could and I knew he would not spare the rod. I've heard him screaming at his daughters, so I knew the rules were no joke.

The first rule was no drugs or going to the clubs alone. I was ok with that because I wasn't into drugs anyway and figured I'd be going out with his daughters at night. Technically, that's two rules but he put them together.

The second rule was no Vespa's. Under no circumstances was I to go on a Vespa because it was too dangerous. I'm not sure I care about a Vespa anyway, so that should be easy to abide by.

The third rule was no sex with boys. Hmm, I kind of hoped Italy would be the place I would lose my virginity, so I'd never have to see the guy again in case something went wrong.

I figured if he was on another continent; I was safe. Another plus was, no one in my town would ever know. This third rule might be rough, but it's not like I was running around with men anyway. By American standards, I was a late bloomer, but my parents would be happy if I remained that way until I was 30.

The fourth rule was if any boy wanted to ask me out, he had to ask him first and the kid can't be a *chooch* [jackass]. Oh boy. This is not the 1950s and no boy on the planet was going to ask Mr. Volpe, who stood at a very intimidating 6 foot 3, if he can take me out for gelato, sex, or anything else, for that matter.

I felt doomed. I was also shocked because I knew his daughters were wild and definitely breaking all the rules. *What did I sign up for?*

We hoped he was being extra tough because he thought I might go wild due to how strict my parents were back home. I agreed to the rules because what else was I going to say? I hoped somehow I'd uncover a way to bypass one or two of these rules and have some fun.

After landing in Italy, we drove from the airport to the Sorrento Peninsula. The hills were alive with stretches of smoke-filled clouds. I later learned many Italians at the time burned their garbage and brush, that created a very distinct smell. How savage, I thought.

To what wild land have I come? I had no idea what I was in for with this trip. My idea of Italy at this point was like a sexy ad with chic women, charming, gorgeous men, and everyone wearing Gucci and Armani.

There would be a lot of butts being pinched and yachting in the clear Mediterranean, while clinking Prosecco glasses and saying, "Cin, cin" all night long. Lord only knows where these images in my head came from.

Driving the coast was long and dizzying. A few times, I had to close my eyes. Hairpin turns with cars speeding in both direction and Vespas racing up in between. Mr. and Mrs. Volpe were in charge of the music which helped me to focus on something other than the twists and turns along the coastline. Most of the time we spent listening to various singers like Julio Iglesias, Luciano Pavarotti and of course, Frank Sinatra.

"Oh, Julio, tell me quando, quando, quando, are we going to get there?' I have a feeling we're going to become very well acquainted on this trip.

The Volpe's loved Julio. I was more of a fan of opera and Sinatra. It's impossible to be an Italian-American and not LOVE Sinatra, Dean Martin, Pavarotti and Tony Bennett, as well as one of my all-time favorites, Louie Prima. All Italian Americans have a working knowledge of Italian opera songs and the big band classics.

I feel so badly for *Medigans* aka Americans. Most have little knowledge of the classics, big band, crooners, or what our families would call "real" music. I'm so thankful I grew up loving opera and identifying with the feelings of the songs and the passion.

Above all, Italians are passionate. Life is not worth living if you're not passionate about a few things. Luckily, Italians have a lot to be passionate about, like food, music, wine, sex, romance, cars, art, love, fashion and creating beautiful things with our hands.

We really are a passionate, creative bunch of people and you don't mess with our creative process. Italy inspires you to create and put love into everything you do.

Winding road after winding road, we had to slow down because you could only go so fast around the mountain. If someone is coming the other way on the blind curves, you either go into the ocean or into the mountain.

There are mirrors sticking out of the mountain, but they only let you see who is going to kill you should you decide to drive too fast. As we slowly drove around one curve, I saw the three infamous, shiny black jetties on my right, off the coast towards the end of the Sorrento Peninsula.

Volare

"Nel blu, dipinto di blu." Domenico Mudugno

Our villa was near the end of the peninsula in an area called Punta Massa. Looking out into the beautiful blue ocean and sky, I immediately understood the song, "Volare." When Domenico Mudugno sings the chorus and says that the sky is painted blue, he wasn't being poetic, but honest. The Mediterranean is the bluest of blues I've ever seen and yes, it looks painted. The skies are also an incredibly brilliant blue. They don't look real.

My eyes couldn't believe what I was seeing. Being a Jersey girl, I've spent half of my life down the shore looking out over the ocean, but this exquisite scene was something I've never seen before. I felt like the world had been keeping this secret from me all my life.

Eventually, we pulled into a parking spot high on the cliff. I thought we were taking a break to catch the view, but as it turned out, this was the roof terrace of the house, as well as the entrance.

We lugged our suitcases towards the stairs that actually go down into the home which had 5 floors. I had a floor all to myself most of the summer. Considering I shared a bedroom with my sister most of my life, this was a palace. Who needs a Vespa? I'm happy right here.

I dropped my suitcase in my room and opened the wooden

balcony doors of the bedroom to the most magnificent sight. Blue ocean, blue sky and black jetties. Below my balcony was a concrete walkway with people sitting on their blankets or chairs tanning. Older men, younger men and kids in speedos with women of all shapes and sizes in bikinis. Ahh, Europe, the land of body-confident people.

I couldn't wait to get down to the water and neither could the Volpe girls. They had already communicated with their friends about our arrival time and they were pulling up to the dock to greet us.

Before we all ran downstairs, I changed into my bathing suit, a sparkly cover-up and a shot of my signature scent, Red by Giorgio. Somehow, that scent always made me feel very chic and like I could be in an Armani ad. Before departing, Mr. Volpe reiterated the rules for me and reminded his girls they were responsible for me. We all pretended to agree with the rules and ran down the stairs, out of the boat-room, onto the docks and into the arms of hot Italian men.

Well, the girls ran into their arms. I kind of waited on the side of the dock until they realized I was there, waiting to be introduced to my newfound freedom.

One guy put his hand out to help me onto the boat. He must have seen the hesitation on my face. Thankfully, this relieved me of potentially slipping and bashing my face on the crisp white deck. As a Jersey girl, I've fearlessly traversed many boats and docks. I guess being the new girl; I was afraid of falling and making the most grand of entrances.

Once on board, it was a total party as the loud music played everything from Madonna to Eros Ramazzotti. I'd never even heard of Ramazotti, but apparently, he was the biggest thing in Italy. His music was very Italian pop, which I did not have an ear for at all.

Every time one of his songs came on, everyone would belt out the song with all their heart and soul. I figured he was the Italian Bon Jovi. Ironically, all over Italy, I saw posters of some hot guy with scruff and super sexy eyes. I later learned that was Eros Ramazotti. Ok, I get it now. Italians were also obsessed with the song "Gloria" by Laura Branigan. I often thought that these people are a little peculiar.

We spent the day sailing, singing, drinking, and of course, eating. I loved it. If this was all I did every day, I'd be ecstatic and have the best summer ever and never come close to breaking the rules.

It seemed like everyone coupled up on the boat. Even though there were a few singles, I was feeling a little on the outside; coupled with a language barrier. I spoke some Italian but not fluently and definitely not fast enough to keep up with fast conversations.

I tried, but I wished I was blonder and prettier to make up for my language deficiencies. Despite the language barrier, I was loving Italy, the men, the food and the freedom. After the Volpe girls got their fill of their summer loves and remembered I existed, we all hung out, jumping and diving off the boat into the water and being silly. Cannonballs are a glorious universal language.

The water was amazing! It was a clear turquoise. Just like the Jersey shore. Not! I don't know if I've ever been able to see my hand while in the Jersey water, let alone my feet. This was heaven and the water was warm. I did not miss that jolt of Atlantic ice-cold water hitting my face. Fighting off borderline hypothermia is the prevailing feeling of swimming and surviving at the Jersey shore.

There were plenty of boats in the water and people would drop an anchor to find the best party spot.

Now I know where Jersey Italians get their love of tanning. It's genetic and cultural. Italians love getting tan, being tan, increasing their tan, greasing up their tan, and comparing tans.

Everyone was perfectly tan, with no lines. They were laughing at us Americans for being so pale and sickly looking because we're always working.

It was like being in a live Nivea tanning lotion commercial. One of the fabulous women on the boat handed me her Nivea tanning lotion with carrot tanning accelerator in it to get rid of my ghostly appearance as quickly as possible.

She nodded at me in a way that let me know she wasn't really being nice but taking pity on me.

"At least it has SPF 4. Maybe you don't burn and look more sick," she said, looking down at me.

What she really wanted to say was, "What a pathetic, poor, ghostly white Americana with no boyfriend." Unfortunately, I have my father's northern Italian skin that goes from translucent to lobster in 10 minutes flat. By the end of the day, I was burnt, and I knew I was going to peel the next day. What a way to start my summer vacation.

After returning to the villa, we ate dinner back at the house and hit the bed with more Nivea cream to calm my skin. Italian skin products are different and more effective than American products. I couldn't understand why we didn't have this stuff in New Jersey. I mean, who likes to tan more than a Jersey girl?

Sleeping in the villa was amazing. Cool nights with the ocean breeze coming through the open balcony doors lulled me right to sleep.

I didn't have a care in the world to keep myself awake. I was tired but also had a serene sense of tranquility in anticipation of my summer of freedom away from my controlling parents. Although Mr. Volpe was pretty strict, there was no comparison to my Bruce Lee skilled octopus-armed, wooden spoon, wielding mother.

It was exciting to see how this summer of freedom was going

to manifest, but I finally had some peace and hoped that this summer was going to be unforgettable. Day 1 was done.

Lemon Heaven

"Quando la vita ti da dei limoni, fa un limoncello."

"When life gives you lemons, make limoncello."

The next day we went to Positano. Mr. and Mrs. Volpe had to meet up with some of the store owners to find out the new trends for the season to bring back to America. The girls and I split up to peruse the shops and check out the boys.

While walking on one of the narrow pathways, I smelled the most amazing lemon smell. It was intoxicating, and I couldn't imagine where or how such a strong smell of lemon could be in the air. I followed the smell, and it led me right to a huge yellow, lemon-scented candle in the doorway of a store called Sapori e Profumi di Positano. Since I love everything lemon, it was like I met my soulmates in the people who owned this heavenly store. Lemon Heaven was the name I called this store, and it stuck with my friends and family.

They had everything lemon you could think of, from perfume to pocketbooks, hand-painted pottery, soaps, tablecloths and best of all; homemade limoncello from the owners' own lemon groves in Positano.

The owners, Sandra and Paolo, were miraculously in the store, giving out lemon candies and sips of their homemade limoncello. She told me the story of how they met and how they started. I was in awe of their love for everything lemon. They were beautiful people and I could actually feel their love with every sip of limoncello and every bite of the candy. I'll definitely be back here before I leave Italy.

I could literally do all of my Christmas shopping for everyone I know, right in this store, without breaking the bank. Their pure ingredients were the very essence of Italy.

I once dated a guy who was appalled my family would give each other home-baked goods, homemade canned foods, or gourmet foods for Christmas gifts. I never even thought twice about it, but he thought we were strange and low-class.

Every year, I loved getting homemade goods, including canned roasted peppers, herb-infused olive oil, cranberry bread, zucchini bread, cookies, homemade mozzarella, canned marinara, wine and any other great food someone was famous for making. I thought this was normal.

My boyfriend thought Christmas gifts should be Louie Vuitton, jewelry or tickets to the theater.

He also ate cheese out of a spray can, so I wasn't going to take his opinion on gifts of food. I love a homemade Italian Christmas. Needless to say; he never made it to Easter time. He would have died when my Aunt Mary-Ann came with the *pizzaghen* or Easter meat pie as my gift every year. It made me happy and isn't that what gifts are supposed to accomplish? If she had handed me Broadway tickets, I would have loved them and I would have been so appreciative and then I would have asked, "But did you make the *pizzaghen*?" You must know your audience. I know all my friends and family would absolutely love to have something from Lemon Heaven.

The Volpes met up with us at Lemon Heaven and, of course, they knew the owners. They bought a bucket of lemon-scented soaps for the villa and extra to take back to the States. These were little lumps of lemon love, to make every shower an homage to Positano. These beautiful memories call out to you forever and ever.

We shopped and ate our way around Positano. We had gelato at Gelateria Buca di Bacco, next to Chez Black, then a gigantic piece of warm *treccia* [a cheese made from mozzarella] and meats from the little grocery store on the corner of the hill followed by a second round of gelato. I was on gelato overload.

How are these people all not 300 pounds?

We walked in and out of every store along the path. One was more exquisite than the next. Most of the stores were way out of my price range, but I couldn't wait to see every store. I felt fabulous browsing and pretending I could afford such craftsmanship.

All that shopping made us hungry again. It's like clockwork that every hour we're hungry. We sniffed out the most amazing piece of grilled buffalo mozzarella that was actually grilled on lemon leaves. This method infuses the lemon into the cheese. It's served warm and matched perfectly with the wine.

We walked back up the hill after lunch, drove back to the villa and tanned with "the boys" before dinner.

Cuori Infiniti

Sei sempre nel mio cuore.

You're forever in my heart.

Every morning breakfasts were on the main balcony off of the living room. We started out with a cappuccino, a cool breeze and a fresh ciambella [doughnut] from the town bakery, where no one spoke English. A ciambella is basically a perfectly warm dough ball rolled in sugar. It's full of warm, inviting joy.

As we sat and discussed the possibilities for the day's activities, Mr. Volpe asked us how "the boys" were. I kind of froze and hoped he wasn't asking me this question, but more toward his daughters. The girls giggled and said the boys were great and how much fun we all had swimming, boating and eating.

He knew most all the boys by name because they were their summer boyfriends, in addition to friends that the girls hung out with every year. The Volpes were in one of the most exclusive social circles on the Amalfi coast. I had no clue who these people were yesterday, but apparently, they were some of the richest kids in the area. Mr. Volpe was friends with bankers, importers/exporters, realtors and store owners. This meant he knew many of the movers and shakers in the area.

No wonder no one was interested in the Albino, plain, average American girl. These guys got the best of the best and the Volpe girls were gorgeous, chic and rich.

I was none of those three things, so I knew I'd have an uphill battle. Italian men can be animals, so I wasn't too worried about eventually finding my summer love.

I'm not looking to discover my true love, just my summer love.

The next day, the Volpe girls and I took a bus to Piazza Tasso in the center of Sorrento to hit the stores and do some serious shopping. There was no thought about what I wanted to buy; aside from my dream of owning a classic Gucci bag. I love the black bags with the red and green stripe. The black Gucci was simple, elegant and unattainable for me.

I was praying I might find one on sale or some rich guy on a yacht would sweep me off my feet with a Gucci and a summer of yachting on the blue Mediterranean. A girl can dream.

The middle of Piazza Tasso is crazy. Between the cars, Vespas passing on the left and the right, people walking through cars and bicycles, it was almost impossible to get from one side to the other.

They named the square after Torquato Tasso, an Italian poet from the 16th century. He had some sort of mental illness and I feel like the craziness of the square might have been how he felt in his head.

High-quality artisans filled the stores with hand-blown perfume bottles, homemade limoncello, inlaid wood items and hand-painted pottery.

The smell of leather, cappuccino and garlic filled the streets. I was officially in love with Italy. This was the exact moment and spot I fell in love with Sorrento, the Amalfi Coast and Italy itself.

Piazza Tasso stole my heart and filled me with the hope of becoming all things Italian this summer, man or no man. Here I am fully alive and all of my senses are fully engaged. I am *pazza* [crazy] for Tasso!

It was a gorgeous, hot and sunny; a typical Sorrento day. Every color was in Technicolor. The shops are colorful and every white lace dress was whiter than snow. Every lemon was more yellow than the sun and every hot pepper was more red than the lava from Vesuvio.

Italy is alive. I love New York; it has its own different energy. It has a more dark underground, frenetic and opportunistic energy. Here, the energy is more light, open and alive; as if Willy Wonka made it for our pleasure. Your heart literally bursts open to let the light and love inside. That's the only way I can describe Sorrento and Positano.

Strolling along the alley, I stopped at a store displaying gorgeous, sexy white lace sundresses hanging from cords attached to the awning. The store owner saw me checking out the dress. He pulled it down and aggressively handed it to me, asking me if I wanted to try it on, but what he was really telling me to do was to try it on. He had a makeshift dressing room with curtains hung from the cords hanging down from the awning.

Since much of his store moved out onto the street for the shoppers, I could see how this dressing room would be easy, efficient and acceptable. As he handed me the dress, he had a look in his eye that immediately made my stomach do a few jumps, and my body froze for a second as we locked eyes.

My body is very sensitive to people with a creep factor or people with bad intentions. It's a gift from God that has literally saved my life many times.

While both of our hands were still on the hanger, I let go and the dress almost dropped from his hand. He looked confused, and I motioned I was sorry and changed my mind.

I knew he was going to watch me undress from the spaces between the curtains of the makeshift dressing room.

Sometimes, it's good to not speak much Italian. I looked around to see if anyone was watching.

I felt like I might need a witness or some help if this guy gets aggressive because he took a dress down and then I changed my mind.

I glanced over to the next store and saw the most gorgeous guy with the kindest eyes, watching everything that was happening. His very discerning eye made me feel as if he was going to jump in any second to save me. Our eyes locked, and he drew me in towards him.

My body immediately turned toward this dreamboat and I started walking. I looked at him with the expression of, "Can you believe what just happened?" We never broke eye contact and as I got closer to him, we both kind of smiled half-crooked smiles.

When I got to the entrance of his store, he put his right hand on my left shoulder and said, "You are-a very wise, eh? You know what he was-a going to do, yes"?

Without breaking eye contact, I responded, "Yes, he is so weird and gave me the creeps" as I visibly shivered the creepiness off my body. "*Schivatz*," I said, and he belly laughed because he never expected this little American using this Italian slang term for someone or something disgusting. We both started laughing and his right hand slid from my left shoulder to the right shoulder as he guided me into his perfume store.

Very slick, but let's be real. My goal this summer was to have someone who looked like him put his arm around my shoulders. My first week is looking really great.

"Do you like perfuma?" he asked.

"Yes, of course, I do. What woman doesn't?"

"Ahh, let me see if I can guess your scent," he said with a smirk and sparkle in his eye.

I must have smiled the most mischievous and devilish of a smile with disbelief, because his aqua-green, blue speckled eyes sparkled as if he knew something about me I didn't. He reached over to a fragrance called *Cuori Infiniti,* put his hand around my left wrist, turned it up and sprayed the perfume on it. I waited for a second, smelled my arm, and refused to let him know how much I loved it. I gave him a stern 'Jersey girl' face and asked him why he chose this specific perfume.

He held my left wrist, smelled it and looked deep into my eyes and said, "The name of-a the perfuma, it means Infinite Hearts. You are a very strong-a woman, with-a blood from the mountains that are high in the clouds. Very smart-a, but you don't let people know this.

You have-a 2 hearts. One, it is for the world and one no one ever sees, intertwined within infinity." Then he drew the infinity symbol on my inner forearm with his finger and tapped it twice. "This-a means you are-a very earthy, a little-a spicy and only a little-a sweet, but deep-a down, like this perfuma." He squeezed his thumb and forefinger together to simulate very little for sweet.

I smirked at him with the universal language of sarcasm and he responded, "So, I pick, Cuori Infiniti, *si* [yes]?"

I couldn't hold my emotions in any longer. I looked up at him and I felt my cheeks rise so high they hit my lower eyelashes.

We were in such a bubble I hadn't even noticed we were standing so close our hips were almost touching. His hand moved from my wrist to my hand, which he was now holding. With any other person in the world, this would have been extremely awkward.

With him, it felt natural like we were old friends and we were sharing our most intimate secrets. Well, he actually was telling me my most intimate secrets. It was so intense; I had to break the energy or else I would have ripped his clothes off right in the middle of the store.

I took a step back, squinted my eyes and said, "How did you know all of that about me?"

So, I am right?

"Hmmm, mayb..."

I could barely get out the last part of maybe before we both started laughing. I know my face must have turned bright red. In a natural reaction, I put my hands out to tap his chest while we were laughing and I shifted my weight, which made me stumble right into his arms. I gasped and tried to stand back upright to pull away out of total embarrassment, but his arms held me with his one hand resting on my lower back and the other in between my shoulder blades.

He was definitely holding me close to him and not letting go, but he was also holding me upright to keep me secure as if we were ballroom dancing.

I could feel his intention in protecting me and literally holding me in high esteem, but also letting me know he wanted me. This also gave me a chance to get a fantastic look into his sexy eyes, which were spectacular. They were definitely green but with aqua flecks that forced you to look twice to see if his eyes were green or blue. Mesmerized, there was no way to hide the pleasure of staring into his eyes.

Those few seconds gave me enough time to think of something to say instead of staring at him like one of his biggest fans.

"Umm, what's your name? I don't know who you are and I'm assuming you work here and don't lure young American girls into some store as the *schivatz* guy next door sets up the girls for you?"

"No, but grazie for the smart idea." His eyes glistened and his one brow raised up the same way The Rock raises his. "I am Enzo," as he raised both his arms up wide and said, "and this is the store of *mi famiglia* [my family]." He lowered his arms, reached for my wrist and drew the infinity symbol on my inner arm and asked with a half smile, "and your name, it is infinity?"

"No, it is not infinity. It's Mariella." I said my name in my best Italian accent, drawing out the Ella part to make it a little more sexy than any American would ever dare to say my name. "My friends call me Ella."

"*Allora* [ok], Mari-ella," imitating my sexy pronunciation, "what are-a you doing in Sorrento and-a when-a do you leave me?"

"I'm on vacation and I'm here until the end of August, so for 2 months."

"And-a where do you stay, Sorrento?"

"No, I'm staying with my friends in Massa."

"Oh, Massa is molto, very nice."

Just then the 2 Volpe sisters came crashing into the store giggling. Neither realized I was in the store, almost touching this gorgeous stranger. As I turned my head and made eye contact with them, they stopped laughing at the same time and a big, silent, empty gap filled the store. They walked over with faces like the cat that ate the mouse.

"Sooo, Mari-ella, who's ya friend?" asked the oldest, Angela.

"Oh, no", I thought to myself. Angela is gorgeous and here she comes eyeing up Lorenzo, who's gonna drop me like a hot pepper for one of the beautiful and sexy Volpe sisters.

"Ladies," I said, "this is Enzo, and he was helping me choose the perfect perfume for the summer."

"I'm sure he was," they said at the same time. I could have crawled right into that makeshift dressing room right about now.

"Come on, let's get some lunch and wine. How old are you Enzo?" said Stella, the younger sister, as if she was about to launch into her 20 questions.

Thank God there are only 2 sisters to drill Enzo. Still, I turned to Enzo to hear his answer, and all 3 of us girls were looking at him, waiting for the answer.

"I'm-a 22 and I go to university to study architecture and work *qua* (here), in my family's store."

"Ok, where are we going for lunch?" I asked, as I almost cut him off to hightail it out of there before he got bombarded with questions.

"We're going to La Lanterna because they have great wine, the best limoncello, pizza and wow, those little fried fish are to die for. I've been waiting all year for those little fried fish," said Angela.

Stella barked, "Ok, *andiamo,* [let's go]. Enzo, nice to meet ya." Stella turned towards me and said, "Come on, it's pretty much across the street and down in the alley. Hopefully, we can still get a seat outside."

As they walked out, I turned back towards Enzo and made the face of "Ok, I have to go before they drag me out." I hugged and thanked him for saving me from the *schivatz*.

We laughed, and I held eye contact, waiting for him to ask to see me again. I was so disappointed as I walked out of the perfume store that he didn't call me back in at the last minute. He didn't seem like a wimp, and he definitely wasn't shy. I wondered what happened. Oh well, there are plenty of fish in the Mediterranean.

Outside, I saw the Volpe girls and caught up with them. While we walked to La Lanterna, they teased me about Lorenzo and how I was blushing and gushing over him. Upon walking into the restaurant's alley, we scored a magnificent table with a view of the shoppers walking along the street.

When the head-waiter saw the Volpe girls, it was like he was seeing his long-lost family. I love this about the Italians. They could have seen you yesterday, but every day it's like they haven't seen you in 20 years. They greet you with such a warm, authentic welcome. No cold, fist bumping or dismissive head nods here.

As soon as we sat down, the girls started drilling me on Enzo. Did we kiss? When are we seeing each other again? How did it happen? On and on, they questioned me. I wanted to be excited but he didn't ask to see me again, so it was a bit of a buzzkill. It was fine because I was more interested in the food than in any man.

The owner brought us some of the best pizza I've ever had in my life and they were right about the little fried fish. Apparently, these little fish are only here in the summer and part of September. They're so yummy and you can eat them like little French fries. Just salty enough with crunch. It tempted me to put them on my pizza.

My first real Italian pizza was, wow! There are no words to describe how good it tasted. In America, I don't eat the crust unless it's from my favorite American pizzeria, Santillo's Pizza in Elizabeth, New Jersey.

Theirs is very similar to this Italian pizza. The Italian crust is thin with a little crisp to it for extra flavor and smokiness. The sauce is light and full of flavor with the best, creamy milky, buffalo mozzarella with basil. I wanted to kiss the chef. I could see why this restaurant had been around for decades and one of my parent's favorite restaurants.

In the meantime, the girls were telling me not to worry about Enzo. Since he knows where we're staying, I would either see him again at the beach or maybe he has a girlfriend. I mean, he is gorgeous and charming. It never even dawned on me he would have a girlfriend. Duh, of course he does. So I guess he really was trying to charm me into buying perfume.

We ate like *gavones*; there's no other way to say it. Unless you say it in English and then you would say pigs or if you were going to use proper Italian and not American Italian, it would be cavone! Dessert was warm chocolate cake, cappuccino and, of course, homemade limoncello. Soon, the waiter returned to our table.

He looked at me and said, "This gift is courtesy of your friend." I assumed he meant Enzo because I didn't have any friends here! He then placed an exquisitely wrapped box in front of me with the most beautiful, thick-textured, embossed wrapping paper that looked like it came right from the Roman Empire. It had some gold, red, and copper with black swirls. The girls were ogling and dying to see what was in the box. I didn't want to even unwrap the gift because it was so beautiful. I wanted to savor the memory of my very first gift from a man in Italy.

The anticipation was killing me. I carefully opened this piece of art, so I could save the paper to give to my grandmother because she always saved the wrapping paper to reuse. She was gonna flip over this paper.

I could feel the heat rushing to my face; everyone's eyes in the restaurant were on me to see what was inside the box. Buried in red satin was the heaviest glass bottle in the shape of an infinity sign.

As I pulled it out, Angela's jaw dropped, her eyes got huge, and she said, "Oh my gawd, Ella, do you know what that is?" She banged her hand on the table and said, "That's it, he wants to marry you. Done."

"Angela, I'm in my 20's, I'm not getting married. What are you tawkin bout?"

"Mariella, do you realize what perfume that is? It's one of the most expensive perfumes in the store. It's like over $400

American dollars. Even though his parents own the store, he can't go around giving every girl a $400 bottle of one of the best perfumes in Europe. What the heck did you say to him to make him give that to you?"

"I said nothing, I swear! I was shopping in the store next to his and I was going to try on this gorgeous, white lace dress, but the sales guy *skeeved* me out, so I went into the perfume store to escape.

Who knew he was so charming and flirty? I thought he was the typical Italian guy everyone talks about. Ya know, I thought he was trying to sell me this; not give it to me. Now what do I do? I have to give this back. We need to go back there now."

Stella raised her limoncello to toast and congratulate me on my soon-to-be wedding and we all broke out laughing. The waiter came back to see what was happening and when he saw the infinity bottle; he made a face of surprise.

He seemed to be impressed with my gift; as if someone thought I was the most special girl in the world and, at that moment, I felt like I was. This gift is working.

The girls and I discussed my next move and what to do. We all agreed they would wait for me in Piazza Tasso while I returned to the store to thank him and return the perfume. They said this move he made was a big deal because all the store owners have been here for generations and they all know each other. Now everyone in the restaurant knows he snuck this gift to the owner to give to me. There is nowhere to hide; I was mortified, but also flattered by Enzo, whatever his last name is.

As I walked towards his store, I was wishing I hadn't eaten those extra slices of pizza because my pants were a little tighter than they were an hour ago. I was thinking of a hundred creative things I could say to sound mature, experienced, mysterious and any other adjective I could think of which would describe a woman someone like Enzo would want to have fun with this summer.

When I walked alone into the store, I asked the girl behind the counter if Enzo was there.

"No, he's out to lunch."

"Ok, well, please tell him that Mariella stopped by to see him."

She nodded at me like, "Yeah, you and a hundred other girls this summer, Americana."

As I tried to exit the store, the streets were so crowded with people, I could barely weave through them to find my friends. The shops line each side of the street and they all have their wares on tables outside of their store. It is two to four people deep in front of each shop, as well as two lines of people trying to walk down the crowded tiny streets. Of course, no one wants to let you in for fear you might buy the same item they're trying to buy. It can be as tight as any nightclub in New York City with people bouncing off each other trying to shop, eat and move. Once I got into the line of people shopping, I got bumped really hard right into some guy. I was so annoyed that I almost dropped my perfume. The man actually grabbed my biceps and stopped me from falling into other people. I looked up and as our eyes met, we both started laughing.

It was Enzo. Once again, he put his hands on my shoulders and guided me back into his store.

"Thank God it's you, Enzo."

"Yes, this is-a my lucky day for sure."

"Thank you so much for this gift. It's gorgeous and are you sure you meant to give this to me? I don't feel right taking it."

As I brought the box towards him, the girl at the counter was staring at me with eyes of fire. I'm surprised I didn't instantaneously combust right there. When she saw the box I was carrying, she knew exactly what it was, and I saw her look at the empty spot on the shelf where it used to be displayed.

She was not happy at all about this pale, average American having this perfume that is reserved for the best and wealthiest women to purchase.

"Ok, I take it back." He jokingly reached out, and I put the box behind my back so he couldn't take it back.

"I already opened it, so I guess I can't give it back. It's so generous and thoughtful and I love it. *Grazie mille,* [thank-you so much] Enzo."

I leaned over and went to kiss his cheek, which wasn't that far since he was trying to reach around my back. As I kissed his cheek, he put his arm around my waist and pulled my hips into his.

He put his other hand around the back of my head and gently grabbed some hair, took a deep breath and said, "Mari-ella, I like you. When can I see you?"

I looked at the necklace around his neck that had the gold letter "L" hanging from it.

To break the tension and try to catch him in some lie, I asked him, "Why do you have an "L" hanging on your necklace?"

"My name is Lorenzo, but everyone calls me Enzo."

Satisfied with his answer, I smiled so I didn't look like a jealous psycho.

"I see you-a tomorrow, yes?" he asked.

I immediately thought of what Mr. Volpe said about boys having to ask to see me.

"Yes, tomorrow. Come down to the house and come on the boat with all of us. A bunch of people have boats and we're going to swim and hang out."

"Ok, Mariella, I will be there. Where am I going?" he asked.

On the back of his business card, I wrote the address and drew a little dragonfly. I mentioned the door of the home has a tile with a dragonfly on it and to ring the bell next to the dragonfly on the bottom floor at the boat entrance. I hoped I could scoot out of the house and hit the docks, so Mr. Volpe would think he was one of the many friends of his daughters.

I gave him my grandmother's famous shoulder lift and said, "*Arrivaderci,* [goodbye] Lorenzo."

He raised his eyebrow and winked at me. I almost died. It was so sexy. Thank you, sweet baby Jesus. I love Italy. Tomorrow can't come fast enough. Meanwhile, the salesgirl's eyes never left us. Her face was so red I thought she was about to explode.

That night, the Volpes and I went to this amazing restaurant in Sorrento that was half inside and half outside. It was in an actual lemon grove with little lights strewn throughout the lemon trees. Italians will put lights on anything and everything. It makes everything magical, romantic, and pretty. This restaurant was no different. The great ambiance matched the great food.

The land in Italy is so rich and the quality of every seed is so pure. Food tastes like it comes right from the Garden of Eden.

Even New Jersey tomatoes, which are the best tomatoes in America, can't touch an Italian tomato. Mr. Volpe did the ordering for the table and I had no problem with that. We ate family style; ordered a bunch of plates we all shared. There is no reason to have only one appetizer, one dinner and one dessert, when you can have a few of each and enjoy many flavors. We drank the table red and table white wine then ended with limoncello and espresso. As we walked around Piazza Tasso, Mr. Volpe smoked his cigar before returning to the villa. I was happy I didn't see Lorenzo and glad the girls let me keep my secret. They knew better and were dying to hear what happened. I couldn't wait to tell them. Another magical day in Italy, *bellissima* [gorgeous].

I could barely sleep while imagining all the different ways Lorenzo was going to kiss me. Sleeping late rarely happened because the early mornings were reserved for the boys playing soccer outside my window. This is where I learned another Italian word, "*spigelo,*" which means edge. I know this because the boys were constantly yelling it as the soccer ball went out of bounds and hit the *spigelo*; right underneath my balcony. In the southern Italian dialect, it sounds like shhhPee-go-lo. I've never forgotten that word, as I heard it over and over every morning that summer.

Apparently, the concrete ledge alongside the ocean was the perfect place to have early morning soccer games.

A Day With Lorenzo

*"'Many times I can't believe the beauty my
eyes are seeing." Lora Condon*

We started our day with another breakfast on the balcony looking at the jetties. I loved watching the fishermen moving their boats out to sea while the little waves hit our dock. I couldn't think of a better way to start the day. Today was the big day. Was Lorenzo going to show or not? While eating breakfast, we listened and sang along to Frank Sinatra and Dean Martin; two of American's favorite Italian American singers.

They've got such depth and emotion in their voices, yet still so smooth. I was especially fond of Sinatra's song; It Was A Very Good Year. Mr. Volpe would take the lower register and the rest of us would sing the upper register. The first line of the song starts by saying that at age 17, it was a good year." Personally, I would never want to go back to 17 because this year is awesome!

Even in the morning, Mrs. Volpe was fabulous with her flowing pareos from Tahiti. Today she had a day of shopping scheduled in Positano. She asked us girls if we wanted to accompany her.

We had to act very bummed about missing out because we already made plans to go boating and swimming. Mrs. Volpe seemed glad she could shop in peace, and I was happy to give her the time alone. I usually loved shopping with her because she would source items for her husband to import for rich and chic American women to buy.

Today, I had better plans. After breakfast, we got ready to hit the docks. I slathered on the SPF for fear of being handed sunblock out of pity. But more so, if I'm burnt to a crisp, it will hurt when Lorenzo hugs me. I couldn't wait to put on some of my new perfume. I even put a little in my hair, so it wouldn't come off when sweating. Priorities.

The doorbell from the boat room rang, and I almost froze. We all got up and said our goodbyes for the day and ran down to the boat room to meet the group of guys and girls.

Thank God Lorenzo was standing with the group. If Mr. Volpe was watching, which I knew he was, to make sure we were all right, it wouldn't look like I had a date. I kissed and said, "Hello" to a few people before I got to Lorenzo. I tried not to bolt right at him because I was so excited.

Lorenzo already knew half the people on the boat. He seemed to play it cool when I was there or watching. Maybe he was trying to hide the fact that he knew all these super-rich people. I didn't realize he was one of them. It makes sense, considering his family owns a tourist shop, but I wasn't even thinking of his status in Sorrento when we met. I wasn't aware there was a whole social structure in Sorrento, Positano and the whole Amalfi coast.

When we met, I could barely put a sentence together, let alone delve into his social status. Everyone seemed to like him and that made me feel much more comfortable. My intuition was correct about him; I felt safe. Every girl knows that feeling of safety when a guy is not playing any games.

As we all boarded the boats, I overheard someone ask Lorenzo where his boat was and if his brother was bringing it later in the day. His brother had to work at the store, so no, he was not coming. I pretended not to hear. I've been around enough rich people to know that as many that like to flaunt their money, there are more that prefer to not flaunt it.

It's not that they don't talk money, but it's more about investing and smart deals, not about the "things" they have. I could tell he wanted me to like him for who he was and not for his standing in the community or money. Sometimes it's nice to be unknown and taken for who you truly are and not the image.

I totally understand that feeling, but only from being on the opposite end of the financial spectrum.

Lorenzo and I sat on the side of the speedboat. The wind was whipping through my hair and almost right in his face.

He leaned over and said, "Mari-ella, you smell so good. I told you that was-a your scent. Drive-a me crazy."

All I could do was smile and grab his cheek to squeeze it. In my nervousness, I mentioned that the *miserab* [miserable], sales girl, didn't seem too happy he gave me this perfume.

Lorenzo laughed hard and said, "Don't-a worry about her, that's-a my sister, Caterina. She hates all-a the girls that come to see me."

"All the girls, huh?" I said, "And just how many girls are coming to see you?"

We both laughed. He actually blushed and had to look away from me. It was so cute and I really didn't care because those girls aren't here right now. I am. We sped through the blue Mediterranean for a while and then, standing right out of the water, were 3 gorgeous rock formations. We anchored and jumped out to swim. Lorenzo pointed to the 3 rocks and told me they are called the Faraglioni of Capri.

The first rock is called Stella and the middle rock has an arch and is called Faraglione di Mezzo. The 3rd one is Faraglione di Fuori. They're all beautiful and iconic, and here I am swimming around them with some of the most beautiful and iconic family names on the Amalfi coast. *La dolce vita* [the sweet life] for sure.

The Mediterranean here looks like glass. Viewing the coast from the water makes one appreciate how beautiful the area is and how cities are literally built into the mountainside. It's so full of life. It's also very peaceful and charming. Last week I visited Seaside Heights, down the Jersey shore where I encountered trashy people, bad greasy pizza, dirty ocean water and jellyfish. This week, I'm hanging out with highly educated, wealthy, cultured, fabulous young people, eating the best pizza in crystal clear water with perfect weather.

While Lorenzo and I were floating on a raft, we talked non-stop about the differences between Italy and America, school, life, and our dreams.

It was amazing how much we had in common, considering our opposite upbringings. At one point, the most beautiful, intense song came on the radio and everyone started singing. I never heard the song before, but they were all so passionate. They made sweeping hand gestures and sang to each other. I had to ask Lorenzo what song this was and what were the words that inspired everyone so much.

He told me it was "Caruso" by Lucio Dalla. Dalla was singing about Enrico Caruso and how he was missing his love as she went back to America.

"Ahh, I see" I said. "Are you going to sing like that for me when I leave for America?" I quickly laughed with embarrassment after saying something so bold.

He put the palm of his huge hand over my cheek and angled my face towards him and said, "I miss you already."

I almost bust out in nervous laughter, but he was so serious. I kept smiling and cuddled into his chest as we floated around the Faraglioni.

After a while, Lorenzo held my face and said, *"Tanto gentile, e tanto onesta pare* [So kind and honest it seems]."

I looked deep into his eyes and said, *"La donna mia, quand'ella altrui salute* [my woman when she greets others]."

His eyes got so big and a look of total shock came over his face. "You know Dante?" he asked.

I shyly responded, *"Si, lo so"* meaning "yes, I know." Little did he know, I was in the Dante Alighieri club in my high school, which was the Italian Club. We studied Dante in old Italian, new Italian, old English and new English. We studied enough of Dante to make my head spin.

Dante helped create and unify the Italian language because Italy was divided into kingdoms and each kingdom had their own dialect until 1861. We were quoting the first few lines from Dante's sonnett in 1290. A little random thing to have in common that definitely made him know there was more than meets the eye with me. It actually made me feel the same about him. He was not just another rich, pretty face.

It became our little love secret. Grazie Dante, *grazie mille* (thanks a lot).

After swimming, floating, singing, and lunch, we headed back to the dock to take a nap and get ready for dinner with Mr. and Mrs. Volpe. I didn't want to leave Lorenzo, and he didn't want to leave me. Towards the end of the day, we were keenly aware that we didn't have that much time left, and we needed to take advantage of every moment together. As everyone was leaving the dock area, he asked to see me later that night. Oh, boy. Here we go. This will be a test if he is really serious or not.

"I know this is weird, but if you want to see me alone, you must ask Mr. Volpe. I'm not allowed to go out with any boys unless he meets them. So sorry."

He looked surprised that I was apologizing and said, "Oh, *si, si*. He is a very smart-a man. My parents say the same to my sister. *Andiamo* [let's go], let's ask," and he smacked my butt to lead me towards the boat room.

We walked up the stairs and I saw Stella and Angela staring with enormous eyes. I motioned for them to come with me to vouch for Enzo if needed.

At the top of the stairs, Mr. Volpe was in the kitchen getting something to drink and I announced, "Hey, Mr. Volpe, this is Lorenzo." Lorenzo immediately took control and started speaking Italian to Mr. Volpe, who also spoke Italian. How he knew, I'm not sure. I knew enough Italian to know that Lorenzo was telling him that his family owned the perfume store off Piazza Tasso and that he came here with his friends today and that he wanted to see me after dinner tonight. I was shocked.

He was such a gentleman, mature and confident. You definitely don't find this in New Jersey. Our guys all acted like Andrew Dice Clay or Beavis and Butthead; while hilarious, I don't want to date them. I was immediately so proud of him. Even though I wasn't thinking of marriage at this age, I definitely knew he was exactly the type of man I dreamed of marrying. He immediately set a very high standard that no other man ever came close to reaching. Ever.

I could tell that Lorenzo impressed Mr. Volpe and he immediately approved of the match; especially since he now knew where he worked if something happened. I was totally relieved. The Volpe girls started talking about how much fun we'd had that afternoon and this "Caruso" song that they knew he would love. We turned on the radio and "Caruso" was playing. Lorenzo translated it word for word, and I know I had to be all starry-eyed. Even Mrs. Volpe came in from tanning on the balcony to listen with us.

We were all singing as loudly as possible and this helped to break the awkwardness for me. "Caruso" became the theme song for our summer. Before Lorenzo left, Mr. Volpe reminded us no Vespas, and that Enzo had to come back and pick me up in a car. *"Si, no problemma, signore"* [Yes, no problem, sir]. We went to dinner, returned home, and I couldn't wait for Lorenzo to pick me up.

When the bell rang, I catapulted from the chair, and everyone started laughing. They knew he was a good guy, and I was finding my Italian magic. They've all had magical experiences in Italy and they knew exactly how I was feeling. The Volpe's were American but met on the beach in Positano in their early 20s. They have returned almost every year since.

The Volpes met the right people in Italy, and now they're a part of the "in" crowd. They're not involved in any of the small-town drama or trying to compete with these millionaires. The Volpes were there to love Italy, the food and the people, while mixing a little business with magic. They made for great friends and Mr. Volpe could dismantle many of the most ego-filled men.

He didn't want their money, their wives, their daughters, or real estate. He only went to source products to bring back to America and have his summer vacation at the same time with his family.

As I bolted towards the door, I stopped short, took a deep breath and fixed myself. I opened the door and saw his beautiful sparkling eyes looking right into me. He came in and Mr. Volpe asked him where he was taking me.

"First to my town square to meet my brother and friends, then gelato, then I return your precious cargo to *la casa della libellula*."

"Casa della what?" I asked.

"*Libellula* is dragonfly," House of the dragonfly, Mr. Volpe responded.

"Ahh, ok, *andiamo* [let's go]." I said, trying to not stay longer than necessary.

"Be back before 1am," Mr. Volpe reminded us.

"Si, signore, no problemma."

While my mother would never let me stay out until 1am in America, in Italy it is normal. Lorenzo opened the door, and I went up the stairs to the roof. There was this little FIAT or as we say in America, "Fix It Again Tony!" He opened the door to my chariot, and I had my first real FIAT experience with my first real Italian, on my first actual date in Italy.

Off we went.

We Speak No Americano

"I consider Italy the front of civilization as we know it today. The Italian Renaissance brought about a richness of intellectual and artistic contributions that have shaped our culture. Aside from art and music, Italians have affected people in more ways than can be measured." Paul Sorvino

In his town's center, we parked right up against the stone wall with the driver's side on the road's shoulder. I had to climb over the clutch to get out on his side because they squeezed us in like sardines. That's totally normal parking for Italy. With the lack of space, it's totally understandable. It's a New Yorkers' parking dream since it doesn't seem like there are any parking rules except don't waste space. We walked towards the town center which was filled with people. At 9pm most suburban towns in America are dead.

It was almost 10pm, and this place was rocking and filled with all ages of people. Everyone was out having fun. They were talking, smoking, eating, drinking, and feeling alive.

I'm guessing his brother and friends hang in the same spot because we walked right over to where they were amid hundreds of people. He introduced me to everyone. Only a few spoke English, so I naturally gravitated toward them and they were excited to say all the English words they knew. They knew mostly curses and asked me all kinds of crazy questions about America and if I'd ever seen any celebrities. The only celebrities I knew were the local Mafia guys.

Every little group of people in the town square had their own music playing on a radio they'd brought with them. Every once in a while, when a group had the best song, all the other groups would turn their music down to sing and dance with the other group.

It was like being in a musical from the 1950s. It was such a wonderful sense of community. In our group, a song came on I never heard before, but it had a fun, upbeat tempo, with a Louie Prima sound. All the boys started singing and got in a big circle closer to the middle of the square and surrounded Lorenzo and me. He took my hands, and we started dancing while everyone was singing. Soon, the other groups gathered around to see what was happening.

I later learned this classic song was called, "Tu Vuò Fà L'americano" [You Want To Be American], sung by Renato Carosone. Everyone was singing and the other people seemed to figure out that I was American, since they all pointed at me whenever he said, "L'*americana*." It made the world a little smaller and, just like that, everyone forever knew me as *L'americana*.

After singing and dancing, we caught our breath and got some gelato. Picking one flavor was not possible, so I got 4 small scoops of each. There was no reason to choose only one. Chocolate, strawberry, pistachio and lemon became my epic combination. I had to have them all! Enzo thought I was nuts, but he's spoiled.

I had limited time here, and I was going to take full advantage of everything. I checked my watch and unfortunately, we only had a ½ hour left before I had to get home.

My first night out and there was no way I could be late getting home. This was my first big test. We jumped in the car and got back with 10 minutes to spare. I can see why everyone has a Vespa. It's simply faster and easier to get around.

We walked down the stairs to the waterside by the boat room and it was pitch black except for the moonlight and some lights from the fisherman's boats bouncing off the water onto his black curls as they brushed against his jaw. It was quiet and romantic and where I hoped I would get my first kiss from Lorenzo.

Once we got in front of the dragonfly tile next to the door, Lorenzo pulled me into him as if we were ballroom dancing and he started singing, "In Sorrento, where love is-a king, when-a boy meets-a sexy girl, here's what they say, that's amore." He dipped me, slowly brought me back up halfway, and kissed me with his eyes open.

I know this because my eyes were open as well. This was pure Italian romance, and Dean Martin would have been so proud. Yes, this is amore. He raised me all the way up and gave me enough of a push toward him, so we kissed again with our eyes wide open. He was so proud that he learned to sing this song in English for me.

I asked him why he kissed me with his eyes open and he confidently said, "I don't want to miss-a this kiss. Why do you kiss me with your eyes open?"

"Because I don't want to miss this kiss," I responded.

We laughed and then he kissed my forehead and smacked my butt to make me go toward the boat room so I wouldn't be late. I'll never forget that kiss. It was perfect and romantic and now I know why he kept a little vial of olive oil in his pocket.

It kept his lips perfectly soft. Good thing I had a curfew or else we would have kissed all night. It felt like I was walking up clouds instead of steps. I couldn't believe this was the beginning of the best summer of my life.

Funiculi, Funicula

This is the story of a disaster like no other. When Mount Vesuvius erupted, it rained seven and a half million tons of debris onto Pompeii. It sealed the fate of more than a thousand people. But it also sealed the city in. Preserved it. Protected it. Like nowhere else on Earth, the rediscovered Pompeii gives us access to the ancient world. And now with new findings and new insights, we can tell the story of the ordinary people caught up in this disaster. (Rome & Archaeology & Volcanoes & Pompeii & Italy) Rome Revealed: Doomsday Pompeii s1e3

I looked forward to the tour of Vesuvius and to see the ruins in Pompeii from AD 79. Ercolano, a town slightly further from the base of the volcano, was also ruined by Vesuvius but left well preserved. Many people don't go there, but it is absolutely worth the extra time.

Approaching the legendary volcano on this big tour bus was making my stomach a little queasy from going around and around the mountain. While I was taking big breaths to calm my stomach, I looked out the window and saw two people having sex on the side of the road. It was pretty out in the open and there is no way they didn't realize everyone in the tour busses would see them as they passed.

They knew people would see them. I also wondered how long it took them to hike up the volcano. The bus drives you halfway up the volcano and you hike the rest. That was my first time seeing people have sex in person. Italians are definitely passionate about their passion.

As we made our way up the volcano, it seemed like we were going up an enormous mountain. The tour guide told us that around 1880 there once was a cable car or funicular that would take people to the top. It was destroyed in 1944 when Vesuvio erupted again. Nothing like a little scare on the way to the top!

To promote the cable car, the song "Finiculi, Finicula" was written and published. I love this song and never knew it was about the cable car that takes you to the top of Vesuvio. This song has sold over a million copies and sung by all the talented singers of the day. Just goes to show that if you have a good hook, you can sing about anything.

Once the bus parked, we got off the bus, and our guide said to us, "You're going to do this once and only once. Go to the top, take pictures and remember it. You will never want to do this again." Suddenly, I wondered what the heck I got myself into.

I was young and in great shape, so I couldn't imagine what he was talking about and figured he was just old. Boy, was I wrong. This trek was easy, however, it was straight up. I was definitely huffing and puffing as I got to the top. When I finally reached the top, I looked down into the mouth of Mt. Vesuvio and thought, "Yup, I'm never gonna do this again." There was no reason to subject myself to this, especially in the summer heat. Interestingly enough, if someone speaks on one side of the mouth of the volcano, you can clearly hear them on the other side of the mouth of the volcano. The sound travels down into the volcano and comes up to the other side.

That was amazing. The thought of lava rushing out of the mountain at 100 miles per hour gave me chills. The image of being buried and burned alive and frozen in time by ash was unimaginable. Ercolano was buried under 50-60 feet of ash. I will never forget touring this area and not just for the people having sex in the woods.

Pompeii and Ercolano are hauntingly spectacular. They developed quite advanced irrigation and sewer systems. They dug deep holes in the ground to keep the water cold and to create ice.

Many lived a carefree lifestyle. To this day, the people living in Pompeii are known for being a little crazy! They very much live in and for the moment, right under the greatest volcano in all history that can erupt at any moment and will again one day.

San Pietro Hotel

"Tuosto, stuorto e cu a' punta" - tough and twisted at the tip

The next day we went to The San Pietro Hotel in Positano for lunch with The Volpes. They said it was chic, so I had to find something fancy to wear. The bad part was I owned nothing fancy and brought nothing chic-appropriate. The good part was that The Volpes knew everyone, so I could definitely get access to the best outfits. Then the bad part was that I couldn't afford half those clothes, let alone the more expensive ones. I think everyone saw my fear when I asked Mrs. Volpe what I should wear and she responded, "Fancy." This wasn't part of the deal for me.

I didn't think I'd need anything fancy, especially in the hot summer at the beach. I guess I'm spoiled in New Jersey where no one dreams of getting fancy down the shore. It's flip-flops and bathing suits almost 24/7.

Mrs. Volpe told me not to worry and that we'd go shopping a little earlier because she knew the best place to get an outfit. I totally trusted her and her style. We drove to Positano and landed at the Cinque clothing store. Mrs. Volpe and her girls hugged and kissed the owner and all the staff as if they were long-lost friends, which they were. While Mrs. Volpe introduced me, she also informed them I needed an outfit for lunch at the San Pietro.

The owner looked me up, down and over, then pulled her glasses down her nose to get a better look. I felt completely naked. She didn't ask me anything about what I liked or wanted. She turned around, picked out a pair of white palazzo pants and an aqua and white one-shoulder chiffon top with a ruffle going from one shoulder across my chest.

One arm was bare and the other arm had long, flowing aqua chiffon with white trim. It fit perfectly and I immediately felt elegant, like I belonged. She saw in my face that I had never seen myself look so good. Her clientele always looks amazing, so watching someone see themselves become elegant and grown up right before her eyes was a welcomed treat.

I was not her typical customer. Immediately, I became one of her staff's favorite clients, because I was truly grateful and allowed them to create my grown-up identity. How blessed was I?

The owner picked a delicate red coral horn or *cornicello* necklace with tiny pearls in the links. It gave the contrast and pop to the outfit. The coral fell right in between my cleavage, so it drew your eyes right to my chest and you couldn't help but look there. A very smart woman. They gave me white sandals with white pearls and a little piece of red coral on the top of the foot to tie into the necklace. The staff told me the red cornicello protected you from the evil eye and infertility. Red signifies passion. The twist in the horn represents the difficulties in life, and that life is not a straight line. The horn has to be a gift to signify that you can't buy your health. I have a gold horn at home like every good Italian, but this was so much more meaningful and special. I figured they knew a lot of the girls were giving me the evil eye because I'm with Lorenzo and they weren't.

I couldn't thank them enough and when Mrs. Volpe went to pay, the owner refused money and said it was her honor to give me my first Positano outfit. I knew what she really meant to say was, my first grown-up outfit. Either way, I was instantly fabulous.

Even the Volpes looked at me differently. Suddenly, I was one of them and I accepted and loved my new role of being fabulous. We were tight on time, so I left wearing my new identity. As we were leaving, we ran into the girl that gave me the Nivea cream on the boat the first day and she barely recognized me. She actually took a step back and her jaw dropped.

She asked what we were doing and the Volpe girls at the same time said, "We're going to meet Lorenzo for lunch at the San Pietro." They couldn't wait to tell her and make her jealous because she always had a crush on Lorenzo. Her face got all scrunched up when they told her and after she walked away, we died laughing.

When we pulled up to the hotel, I immediately understood what they meant by fancy. This hotel is like something you would see in a Frank Sinatra or Audrey Hepburn film. It's epic and the views are spectacular. As we walked to the balcony located right off the lobby, the owners, their family and the management staff came to greet the Volpes.

They immediately gave us Prosecco with strawberries. This combo quickly became my favorite drink. As the Volpes were talking and drinking, I removed myself to go to the restroom.

After exiting the restroom, I saw Lorenzo in the lobby, walking towards the balcony. He turned his head towards me and immediately stopped and looked at me with a smile from ear to ear. I was trying to play it cool, but my look was so dramatically different from the clothes he had previously seen me wear, I couldn't pretend I owned these clothes.

"Wow," he said as we moved closer to each other. "You look-a mazing! You're so beautiful, *molta bella* [very beautiful]. Every man here is-a jealous. But you, you are with-a me; I am-a so blessed."

He cupped his hands together, shaking them as if thanking God, and then kissed my hands and repeated, "So-a blessed."

"Yes, you are. We are," is all I could think of to say in the moment.

He couldn't keep his hands off of me and I had to remind him that the Volpes could easily see us and they know the owners. He joked he knew the owners as well and that I shouldn't worry so much because Italy is all about love. Since we just met, I never really saw this side of him and he definitely had a distinct look in his eye. I knew this look. It was the look of devouring me; I was sending him over the edge.

All I could think to myself was that I needed to buy the entire inventory of the Cinque store. Who knew clothes could have such an effect on a man? I wish I had known this earlier. I had to kiss him and let him nuzzle on my neck a little before we returned to the balcony.

Upon our return to the balcony, the owners and staff all greeted Lorenzo with open arms and traditional European kisses. Mr. and Mrs. Volpe were impressed with Lorenzo's class and charisma with adults.

He could also hold his own with the best of the best in Positano. Both Volpe's were brilliant, talented and accomplished. Mrs. Volpe had a knack for spotting future trends in retail and Mr. Volpe was the stable conversationalist. A true man's man without the machismo that is such a turnoff to other men, as well as women. Together, they were a perfect match for business and relationships.

They seated us on the balcony with the best view. The food was over the top for lunch.

I became aware I was the only one sitting in complete awe of our surroundings and what we were eating. This was a bit of a shock to me. I was experiencing life as a wealthy person and I was far from wealthy.

It was totally out of my comfort zone, but a zone I was very comfortable learning more about and staying in as long as possible. How the heck can I go back to school and care about the mean girls or get $2 tacos, after eating melon wrapped with prosciutto, incredible Italian wine, limoncello, and guests of the owners of a 5-star hotel in Positano? Life seriously can't get any better than this.

Normal people don't eat like this. Fresh, warm *treccia* [braided buffalo milk cheese] with juicy red tomatoes with olive oil from a nearby farm. I ordered squid, black ink spaghetti with *vongole* [baby clams], tomatoes and garlic. I never heard of this before and I was on a mission to have real Italian food, not American Italian. Of course, I love my mom's cooking and traditions, but this was next level.

I wanted to immerse myself in the culture and become even more Italian, if that was possible. Aside from the pretty color, squid ink has nutritional benefits like proteins, amino acids, minerals, antioxidants and even a little dopamine. With traditional foods, I believe Italians have a superior knowledge of health, the body and how to use their surrounding environment to maximize health.

As the centuries go by, we forget why our ancestors used these original ingredients and why they did the things they did, but they definitely had a reason for every meal and ingredient.

Enzo was charming and everyone saw why I was so interested in him. Thank God they were comfortable with him and me spending time together.

This was extremely important for the success of our summer romance. I respected the Volpes very much and would not dare date anyone they didn't approve of. I'm not the type to obey rules because those are the rules, so the rules need to make sense to me and be logical. I wouldn't date someone they didn't approve of, because that's how much I cherished, respected and believed in their judgment. I knew they could see things I couldn't see based on their experience.

As lunch ended, we said our goodbyes and one of the staff members at the San Pietro told me how lucky I was to be dating Lorenzo. She told me he does not bring around women, and that they know him as a very serious boy that I should not let go of, ever.

I assured her I was happy to be with him and I appreciated his seriousness. It was a strange interaction, but I could see she was coming from a place of love, not a place of jealousy or a busybody. She was truly happy for us and could see and feel the chemistry between us. We actually got the same comments from a few different people. Even though we just met, people were noticing the palpable chemistry between us, especially the people that knew Lorenzo.

They had never really seen him give one girl so much attention in public. Italian men don't show off the bimbo to important people at respectable events. His attention, time, and openness with me put me on another level in these social circles.

I was actually feeling the pressure of having to keep up the charade of fancy clothes, fancy meals, and high society. It intimidated me and made me want to pull back from him because I knew I couldn't keep up with generational, old money or even new money.

Mi Dispiace

"Chocolate says 'I'm sorry' so much better than words. Rachel Vincent

Before the sun set that day, Lorenzo and I swam out to the jetties by the villa. We talked and kissed and did what we could on the jetties without breaking any bones, falling off the rocks, or getting too many black and blue marks from the rocks poking into our bodies.

I slipped and told him how I was feeling uncomfortable about his status in society and how I'm not a part of that world. I don't have the clothes, the body, the hair, the face, attitude and most of all, the money to fit in with high society.

He looked at me like I was insane. I know I was only there for the summer, but I don't enjoy looking like a fool, thinking I'm something I'm not.

He reassured me I was being ridiculous, and no one is thinking I wasn't worthy of being with him. Well, no one except his mother. She would change her mind as she got to know me better, I hoped. I told him how I could feel everyone looking at me and wondering how I got to be with him, considering he could get any girl he wanted. Enzo jokingly reassured me that yes, he could get any girl he wanted and had plenty, but they left him bored. He always knows how to laugh me off the ledge.

Most of these girls know they're going to marry someone from their social group, so they act stupid and take a good man for granted.

A solid, loving cherished relationship is not as important as keeping the status going, making the other girls jealous and eventually making their parents proud of their choice in marriage.

I wondered whom his parents wanted him to marry and whom he thought he was going to marry. I'm sure it would be the Nivea girl if his mother had her way. Americans aren't thinking about whom they're going to marry very much in their 20s. For Italians, they think about marriage much earlier; especially when they're wealthy and have a reputation and business to protect. Ah, the joys of high society.

Enzo always knew the right thing to say and how to reassure me. I wasn't lacking confidence necessarily, but I was so out of my element and completely understood these people were in a whole other league I knew nothing about. I believe this was something he was looking for in a relationship.

He wanted someone completely different and someone who didn't understand his social circle or even want to climb the social ladder. He could be his real self with me, and that was a first for him.

On the rocks, he kissed my face and neck inch by inch and tickled me just enough so I wouldn't roll off the rock into the water. He thought it was so funny. If I had fallen into the water, though, I'm pretty sure it wouldn't be so funny.

There is no way to fall into the jetties and not hurt yourself. He was definitely being a *skuch* [pain in the butt] because he kept playing with my wet hair and it was getting twisted. He kept opening and closing the clip in my hair to make a clicking sound.

I told him to stop so my favorite and only clip I brought to Italy wouldn't break.

As we balanced on the rocks, the waves kept getting bigger and started to crash higher on the rocks and smacked in between the rocks. Sometimes it would spray up into our faces and it felt so refreshing. It was incredibly romantic and reminded me of that famous beach scene in *From Here to Eternity*.

As the sun was setting, it was that magical time of the night filled with all the hope, romance and love the day had to offer young lovers. The beautiful pinks and oranges filled the sky as if God painted it, exclusively for us.

While he was playing with my hair clip, I felt my hair fall to my sides and I saw his face freeze under the encroaching moonlight. "What"? I said. He had a strange look on his face. It was a face of fear.

He looked over my head and mumbled, "*Mi dispiace,* Ella, *mi dispiace.*"

"What?" I asked again.

He looked into my eyes and quietly repeated, "*Mi dispiace.*"

"What does that mean, Lorenzo? "

"It means, I'm sorry Mariella, I dropped-a your clip in the rocks. The wave came and I think it has-a gone out to-a the sea with-a calamari."

"Oh, Lorenzooooo, I told you to stop messing with it! I loved that clip and I didn't bring another one. It was the clip my mother brought back from her last trip to Italy." I tried to sound a little more sad than I actually was to make him feel bad.

This clip was the perfect size and strength to hold my heavy, crazy curly hair. It's a small thing, but something that made my life easier and worked every time.

"You owe me a clip and I just happened to see a beautiful one at Cinque's in Positano," I half jokingly mentioned.

He laughed the laugh of defeat and said, "Ok, we go back to Cinque's, you win."

Yes, I get to go back; I thought to myself. I'll never forget learning this word, *mi dispiace* and there are worse ways to learn the phrase "I'm sorry" I suppose. That was our queue to leave and head back to the villa for the night.

As summer progressed, we spent most of our days on the boats with friends. Every day was perfect. Seeing the coast from the water is the most beautiful way to see the Amalfi Coast. So much life that is built right into the mountain. From far away, it is so deceiving and looks like a flat postcard.

It's not until you are in the middle of it that can you see all the dimensions and intricacies of the vibrantly colored architecture. When boating, we would all meet somewhere in the ocean, drop anchors and swim, drink, eat and sing. La dolce vita was all I could think about.

While walking around town, I saw so many people drinking these cold, bright orange drinks. I had to know what it tasted like, so I had one of the guys make one for me.

I drank it so quickly he had to make me another right away. It was called an Aperol Spritz. The drink has Prosecco, a splash of soda, Aperol and a slice of orange. It tastes as good as it looks. Bright, fresh, bubbly and refreshing.

No wonder this bitter and sweet orange mixer with herbs has been around since 1919. I have to remember to bring a bottle of this back home; I thought to myself.

Although I was not into the high society thing, I was able to enjoy the benefits of money.

Having Lorenzo and the Volpe girls helped to ease into their social circle. Many of the girls who weren't jealous of me dating Lorenzo were very nice.

The guys were all nice because I could still potentially be their girlfriend. In reality, I kept Lorenzo occupied so their girlfriends wouldn't wander over to his empty arms. The girls who had boyfriends were happy that I was becoming madly in love with Lorenzo, and not after their boyfriends.

The single girls who wanted Lorenzo were not nice at all and were relentlessly talking behind my back, trying to make me look bad. Their plans backfired because it was plain to see that Lorenzo and I had some major chemistry. With his friends, I always acted with gratitude for their hospitality and never started fights or acted catty. I respected their boats, helped to clean them and clean the plates after lunch.

There was no way I could contribute financially to the party food and drinks. I always did what I could to show my appreciation and for Italians, that's better than gold. It also meant a lot to Enzo. People not only liked but respected and accepted his girlfriend, no matter what. We all fit very well together.

Dating Enzo made the other guys want me. Knowing that I was not annoyingly shallow and ungrateful made them want me even more. Lorenzo was well aware, but I played a little dumb. I had to tell a few of his "friends" that I was not interested in cheating on Lorenzo. Let's face it; if I wasn't dating Lorenzo, these men wouldn't give me a second look. Men will always try, I'll give them that.

One day, while boating, one girl from our group Giovanna, was getting seasick. I felt so badly for her because we were too far out to turn around.

There she was puking over the side of the boat on and off for 20 minutes. We all went over to help her at some point. One of the guys named Giovanni went over to help and actually pinched her butt instead, as she was bent over the side. I thought I would die. In America, this guy would get smacked upside the head by almost everyone. Here, this was normal. He helped to take care of her and they ended up dating. Imagine that.

That's a dating technique I've never seen before and not sure I ever want to see again. That's how men can be in Italy. They have no shame in professing their affection and can be quite aggressive. They don't waste time and I guess, why should they? Life is short. His timing might have been off, but in the end, he got what he wanted and she got someone who still wanted her at her worst.

On our way back to shore, we were going slowly because the water was a little choppy and Giovanna couldn't take anymore.

All of a sudden, we saw a woman standing on a rowboat, rowing toward us. We heard her screaming a name but couldn't make it out very well until she got closer. She was yelling, "Annn-ge-looooooo." It was the same voice and whine that Lucy used when she would cry, "Ricky."

Angelo's name was drawn out into many syllables. I did not know this girl in the boat, but she looked and sounded disturbed, distraught and desperate. All the people on the boats started laughing, but I was confused.

Enzo giggled a bit, but I could see the look of pity and sympathy on his face as well. As they were laughing and pointing, I had to ask him about this girl.

Her name was Marta. She was a lower-class, trashy girl that a few of the guys would pass around. This time, she was coming for Angelo.

He led her on before the summer and then dropped her as all the girls came back from the University for summer break along with tourists. She was making a complete fool of herself, rowing out into the ocean to plead her case and to show her love for Angelo.

He couldn't care less and was laughing the loudest at her. I felt bad. It was sad and pathetic.

"She did it to-a herself, sleeping around in this small circle of men," Lorenzo said, "There is-a no way he would-a marry her unless she is-a pregnant and even then."

I blurted out, "Oh, God, is she pregnant?"

We looked at each other, contemplating the potential of that happening. Enzo looked over to Angelo and said, "I don't know, but if-a she is, oh, his parents will-a kill him. He will have-a to give her money and probably marry her to keep-a the family name-a clean. His father is-a one of the biggest wine exporters in-a southern Italia."

I asked Enzo if it was possible that he loved her?

"Angelo like-a the *pazza* [crazy] girl, so maybe. She is-a desperate for attention and needs to marry rich."

As Marta got closer, we could see her makeup was running down her face from crying, her nose was all red and her once flowing, cream-colored silk dress was wet and it stuck to half of her body like a wave came up and hit one side of her. The saltwater matted her frizzy and fried blonde hair and her black roots looked tortured. She was standing in the rowboat and rocking all over the place. I swore she was going to fall out of the boat. She kept screaming his name in drawn out syllables, "Annnn-ge-looooooo, *ti aaammm-ooooo, ti aaamm-oooooo* [I love you]."

When she was close enough, she stopped rowing and Angelo put the boat in full throttle to speed off. Marta fell backward in the boat with her paddle falling in the water as her boat bounced around in our wake. Her paddle floated away. I felt like I was in a movie. Everything was so dramatic.

They were all laughing at Marta. I took a serious note to never be like Marta. I would rather these girls dislike me because I'm poor or with Lorenzo than pity me for behaving so desperate and pathetic. On our way back to the shore, Angelo's friends eventually did let him know he was wrong to lead her on like that. He swore he didn't, but it was too obvious.

Marta was hurting and believed he loved her. Angelo had dumped her without giving her a second thought so he could play his options this summer.

That afternoon Enzo told me to come to his store to meet him for lunch. I was happy to oblige him because I love the center of Sorrento even though it is touristy. I love the colors, the smells, the gorgeous white lace and red coral jewelry.

The bright yellow lemons against the royal blue and white hand-painted tiles were mesmerizing. Things were starting to heat-up between Lorenzo and me. We were spending a lot of time together. It was going by too quickly. The Volpes were also going to the Sorrento center to do some business, so we all went together and agreed to meet back home.

When I finally arrived at the store, Lorenzo greeted me with the biggest hug and sweetest kisses. "*Mi amore*, follow me" he said, as he grabbed my hand and led me out of the store into an alley. He brought me to his red Vespa and handed me a helmet.

"Um, Lorenzo, I'm not supposed to go on a Vespa. Don't you remember what Mr. Volpe said?"

Lorenzo put the helmet on me, tightened the chinstrap and said, "Then you better hold on-a tight."

He picked me up by the waist and plopped me on the back of his Vespa. I lifted my skirt up as he hopped on and we zipped through the narrow streets of Sorrento to the famous Sorrento Palace Hotel. When we parked, he got off first and then lifted me off the back.

"I'm in so much trouble," I said as he unhooked my chinstrap.

"Don't-a you worry. You don't have to worry about the *Signore*, but you do need to worry a little about meeting *mamma mia* [my mother]. My father will love you. *Mamma mia*, she doesn't like any girls for me."

"What do you mean? Your parents are here waiting for us to have lunch? Lorenzo, oh my God, I look horrible and I have helmet hair. You should have let me know. What do I say? I can't believe you didn't tell me."

"Mariella, you look-a beautiful. Be you. I help. The food here is bellissima [extremely beautiful]. Trust me, *facia bella* [beautiful face]." He grabbed my face to kiss me. Gave me a once-over look and jokingly said, "eh, maybe you should worry, just a little."

"Lorenzooo," I whined as he grabbed my hand and pulled me into the lobby.

Under any other circumstances, I would have been so relaxed and happy to be here. This should make for an interesting lunch. He led me through the hotel, past the six connecting pools. Yes, there are actually six cascading pools in the back of the hotel. I never saw anything like it. The tables surrounding the pools were looking right at Vesuvio.

I spotted a table with two people sitting looking at the water and we wound our way to that table. Introductions were made, and it was exactly as I expected. His father was gracious, warm, smiling and happy. His mother had the emotions of a stone. She might as well have been a German soldier with that stern look and steely eyes. Again, I called on Padre Pio to help me out and make a miracle out of this potential disaster.

I tried to act grateful for being taken to lunch at such a beautiful place, but also to not act like I'd never been to a place so upscale before. I was so nervous and I figured it might be better to say less during our first meeting. His parents dressed impeccably, as did Lorenzo; especially since he was working.

They asked all the basic questions parents might ask the girl that their son brought them to meet. I think they thought I might be too young for him, but they seemed satisfied with my college plans in America. After I said this, I saw his mother's eye go immediately to Lorenzo as if she was saying, "See, she is leaving you, so don't get any ideas about going to America or keeping this affair going; end it now!" I know a mother's look, that's for sure. She was right. I was going back to America.

There was no sense in getting too close, falling in love or keeping this thing going, but we couldn't stop ourselves either. The remainder of the lunch wasn't totally awkward, but there was an underlying feeling of the reality that the Atlantic Ocean would soon come between us. Forever.

Food in Italy is like having an extra person at the table. It speaks to us and we answer. Every bite commences the most magical conversation. We started with cantaloupe wrapped with prosciutto and buffalo mozzarella with tomatoes, basil and a few drops of balsamic vinegar. It was pure heaven.

The combination of prosciutto and melon was perfection. Sweet and a little salty. These are my people for sure. Next came *frutta di mare* [seafood salad], with the most juicy, fresh fish. This dish is a gift from the sea and every time I looked out at the ocean, I was so grateful for the gift.

This is one of my favorite dishes. Crab, octopus, shrimp, squid and muscles. It reminds me of our big family dinners with crabs and fish we would catch off the docks in Forked River, New Jersey. We all split a bottle of red wine from the Campania region and a *focaccia caprese* [bread with mozzarella, basil, and tomato]. They indulged me with red wine after Lorenzo told them I much preferred red over white. We ate family style, so we didn't have to choose only one thing to eat. We ordered a bunch of plates and shared them. This is the way food was meant to be eaten. Like love, it should be good, plentiful, and shared.

I tried to keep the conversation light. His father was fabulous, and I can see from where Lorenzo got his charm and loving personality. Lorenzo knew how his mother was, and I think he wanted to get the first meeting out of the way. The hotel owner came over and warmly greeted us with homemade limoncello. I felt so fabulous and special even with his mother's evil eye upon me. Where is my *cornicello* when I need it? The owner couldn't have come at a better time.

He was very gracious and asked me what I'd done so far and if I liked his food. I gushed over everything. He was so happy as if he was still unsure about his food in the most humble of ways. Food is love. At the most luxurious level, food is art. This hotel and restaurant is one of the most legendary places to stay in Sorrento.

The owner sat with us for a while and distracted Enzo's mother enough for her to forget my presence. I was not upset about being ignored at all.

It was time for Lorenzo to get back to work, so we got up to say goodbye. We exchanged pleasantries and when his dad kissed me goodbye, he held my hands, squeezed them, looked into my eyes and said, "You're a good girl. Such a good girl. I like you."

It made me feel so good. We smiled and looked into each other's eyes. I knew he was happy that I made his son happy enough to bring a girl around to introduce to them.

Dads know what it will take to make another man happy with his wife and stay faithful. Moms, on the other hand, have an agenda about what they think their son should do; not what actually might make him happy in marriage. It was all about appearances for his mother. Appearances, status, and social climbing were her agenda. His father's agenda was happiness.

When I let go of his father's hands, I turned towards Lorenzo's mother and she was looking at us like she couldn't wait for me to leave so she could talk about me. I did the proper thing and kissed her on the cheek goodbye, then rushed to Lorenzo's side to get out of the line of fire.

As we were walking back through the lobby, I looked up at Lorenzo and said, "Well, I think I survived."

He squeezed my hand and said, "You were great, *mi amore.* No worry, mamma mia is-a tough, but good. My father can see your heart, and he knows how I feel."

I couldn't resist, but I had to ask him, "And how DO you feel?"

We stopped at his Vespa and he looked me directly in the eye and said, "I am loving you this much." He pulled out a beautifully wrapped gift from his Vespa pouch and handed it to me.

"Hmmm, I wonder how much," I said as I unwrapped the gift. Once opened, I could see it was the beautiful hair clip from the Cinque store. It was a purple, pink and silver rhinestone dragonfly.

"Awww, Lorenzo, no more mi dispiace," I teased and hugged him so tightly.

When I let go, he said, "And now, you go to Cinque and you buy whatever outfit you want for tonight."

"What's tonight?" I asked because I didn't remember any plans.

He confidently said, "Tonight we are going to Positano for dinner and dancing. The store has some outfits for you to try. Pick one, wear it tonight, and I'll pick you up after work."

I looked at him, kind of confused, and said, "Ok, but how am I getting there and back to Massa?"

"Bella." he said, "that car right-a there is-a for you. The driver take you, wait-a for you and return you to Massa. Have-a fun and take-a nap because you going to need it," he chuckled.

I was in shock. He asked me if I was ok because I must have had a look of shock on my face. I was speechless, which never happens. "Yes, I'm ok, just shocked. Are you sure?" I asked.

"Si, mi amore," he said, and kissed my forehead.

Wow, these are the fun things that money can buy. Yes, money can absolutely buy happiness, because I don't think I've ever been so happy in my life. Actually, I know I've never been so happy. The only event that comes close to this that I can think of was when the Yankees won the World Series in 1977 and 1978. Not too many things can trump Reggie Jackson and Bucky Dent.

As I got into the car with my driver, I blew Lorenzo a kiss. He winked at me and zipped off on his Vespa. The driver took me as far as he could in Positano, parked and escorted me to the Cinque store.

Waiting for me were the lovely saleswomen and the owner. As always, there was a chilled Prosecco waiting for me. I felt like a princess and I was quickly becoming The Prosecco Princess!

As he said, they had a few gorgeous outfits waiting for me. They were all giggling and very excited for me. They kept asking me what we were doing tonight and that tonight must be a very special night if he was buying me a dress. I told them I didn't know.

He surprised me a half hour ago with all of this. They quickly brought me into the dressing room so I could try on the outfits. They made me come out and twirl around in each outfit to see how it would move when I danced the night away. Each outfit had its own jewelry. They played around with my hair, looking for a style that would complement the dress.

They were making such a big fuss over me and then it hit me. Oh no, he wants to have sex. I suddenly froze and felt so insecure. I was totally embarrassed because they had already figured it out. It would be my first time with Lorenzo, and they knew exactly what he had in store for me this night.

After catching my breath, I immediately grabbed the manager and took her into the dressing room to tell her what I thought was about to happen.

She grasped my hands and said, "Ella, I would trust my very own daughter with Lorenzo. He is a good man. You should be happy he cares so much for you. He wants to take care of you and make this special for both of you. I'm not your mother, but...."

"Oh, *Madonna mia*, my mother would kill me if she thought I was going to have sex with some guy in Italy on vacation that I'm never going to see again. I'm under strict rules to not to have sex on this trip. How can I do this?" I asked.

She chuckled and said, "With Lorenzo, I'm sure it will be very easy! You'll be fine. Relax, he loves you."

"How do you know he loves me?" I begged her for reassurance.

"I know he loves you because he can have any girl up and down the Amalfi Coast and he chose you. He never brought a girl to meet his parents. He's never brought a girl here to buy her gifts and clothes or to any other store. I know everything around here. I also heard about that perfume he gave you."

"How do you know about that?" I shockingly asked.

"Ella, all of us families have known each other for generations. We watch, we listen, we talk and we care. If you let Lorenzo lead, you will have the best summer of your life and your mother will get over it. Italy is magic and if you say, 'No,' you might regret it forever."

I had no choice but to agree. She was right. Isn't this what I wished to happen this summer? Enzo has gone out of his way to care for me. No American boy has ever done anything close to this. I never thought I'd be this scared about being with a guy, but all of a sudden, I was very afraid. I felt very insecure and unsure.

She let me sit alone in the dressing room for a few minutes while I contemplated the magnitude of the situation. I had to give myself a little pep talk. As I was talking to myself, I looked up to see the last outfit.

It was the most spectacular white lace dress with shimmering opalescent silk strands woven throughout the lace. It was truly dazzling. I quickly removed the other dress and carefully put the white lace one on. It fit perfectly and it was definitely sexy, but not over the top. It was classic and timeless.

When the light hit the sparkle, it was magical. The A-line cut fit snugly around my waist and made my chest look bigger, which isn't such a bad thing. The length was a little above knee and the skirt part had a little pleat to make the perfect twirls when I twirled around. Yes, this is the dress that he will never forget and neither will I.

When I walked out of the dressing room, everyone in the store stopped. I looked at the manager and she actually had tears in her eyes. "Oh, yes, this is the dress. It's *perfetto* [perfect] Mariella, ahh, *perfetto*," she exclaimed with joy.

"I love this dress," I said as I gave a twirl in the middle of the store.

As I gave another twirl, I stopped halfway and ended up staring right at Lorenzo's mother and her glaring face. I froze and looked at the manager and salesgirls. We all froze for a second and then they all jumped to greet her.

She looked me up and down and said, "I'm surprised to see you here. Is this the type of store you usually shop in back in America?"

"Sometimes, yes," I nervously answered, "but you know, vacation shopping is always so much more fun."

I hoped that would get her off my case. God forbid if she knew Lorenzo was buying me this outfit. She would definitely know exactly what that meant. She was a woman of the world, so there was no getting over on her. Quickly, the owner came out and distracted Enzo's mother, so the girls could get me some jewelry and sandals to match the dress.

They quickly wrapped up the dress, and I thanked them for their help. I told his mother and the girls that I had to go to meet the Volpes back at the villa and that I would see them all soon. I thanked his mother again for a lovely lunch and it was so nice to meet them since Lorenzo is always saying how much he loves them both. It couldn't hurt to kiss a little butt to make nice. She pursed her lips as if to say you're dismissed and I was happy to oblige her. I scooted out of there and headed back up the mountain with the driver.

Back in Massa, I begged the Volpe girls to meet us in Positano at the club, even though I wasn't sure which club Enzo chose.

I figured it was the club right on the beach, but would let them know when Lorenzo came to pick me up. They were dying to know what was happening with Lorenzo, so I had to show them my new dress. When I pulled it out of the bag, they both looked at each other and started screaming at me.

"Oh my Gawd. Oh my Gawd. Oh my Gawd. Do you know what this means? Oh my Gawd, he's gonna give you the hot beef injection. He's gonna give you his pepperoni stick, his Roman gladiator sword. Oh yeah, he totally wants you, Ella."

I was already nervous and now freaking out.

"Guyyyyssss, stooooop it. You don't know that" I whispered in case the Volpe's came home.

In unison they said, "Oh, yeeees we dooooo."

"He has the hots for you and look at all the gifts he's given you. Guys don't do that unless they want some." Stella said.

"I know, but he's so sweet and so good to me and I really, really like him." I said in a dreamy voice.

Angela barked, "Hey, Ella, just do it with him! Get it out of the way. He's a good guy and if something goes wrong, he'll be on another continent and no one will know!"

Stella laughed.

I nervously said, "Wrong? What can go wrong?"

We all laughed and then went into full planning mode on how to make sure the Volpes (specifically, Mr. Volpe) didn't find out and ship me back to America before the end of the summer. We decided that the girls and their boyfriends would meet Lorenzo and me at the club and then he would take us all home in his car, so we would all arrive home safely; together. No lying involved, just the potential omission of some details they don't need or want to know.

As I got dressed for the evening, I was careful to look at every inch of my body and outfit to make sure it was perfect. Shoes, tan, smooth oiled legs, twirling dress that fits perfectly, dewy make-up, topped by curled, not frizzy hair.

The only thing left was perfume. I sprayed a few pumps of Cuori Infiniti into the air and walked through the perfume cloud into the next chapter of my life. As I strutted into the living room, the Volpes were all stunned at my dress. They never asked if I used my own money to buy the dress and I did not offer any info.

I didn't want them to think that Lorenzo and I were that close. They might suspect we either were having sex or he wanted to have sex. Men don't usually buy women expensive things unless they want something or they're getting something in return and we all know what men want. Either scenario didn't look good for my ability to adhere to the Volpe rules.

Lorenzo came to get me and rang the bell at the upstairs door, where he parked his car. "Showtime," I said to Angela and Stella with a very nervous smile. I opened the door and his facial expression was priceless.

It was one of deep love, respect, longing and lust all rolled into one. He cupped my face in his hands. His palms were on the sides of my jaw and his thumbs on my lips and said, "You look like a magical angel sent from heaven for me."

I put my hands on his chest and pulled the collar of his shirt to pull him into me and said, "And I'm all yours."

He groaned and dropped his hands down to my shoulders, then roamed over my breasts, down the sides of my waist, over my butt, down my thighs and back up again. When his hands came back up, they stopped on my butt cheeks and he lifted me up. I flung my legs around his waist and we kissed, giggled and hugged.

We finally went downstairs and sat with all the Volpes on the balcony while Mr. Volpe smoke his cigar, listening to Julio Ingelsis as usual. Enzo stepped right in as if he was a part of the family and knew them for years.

He gave Mr. Volpe some cigar advice about Tuscan cigars and where to get good Cubans in Sorrento. Mr. Volpe was all over that information because he loved getting the local insider tips. Enzo asked Mr. Volpe if he could take me around on his Vespa sometimes. It would be easier for him to not have to go back and forth from work to his house to pick me up. Parking is difficult with a car late at night on the street and in the piazza. Mr. Volpe knew parking in Italy can be a nightmare, which is why even the very old have Vespas in Italy.

"Yes, that's no problem, Lorenzo. Be careful and don't drive crazy when she is with you. Remember, if you break it, you buy it," Mr. Volpe said, laughing loudly at his own joke.

Enzo quickly responded, "Yes, I am already paying."

I playfully backhanded him in the gut and said, "Oh, well, that one is gonna cost ya. Don't worry."

We all had a good laugh, and I told the Volpe girls we'd see them at the club after dinner. We reassured Mr. and Mrs. Volpe that he was going to return all of us together in one piece in a car. This made Mr. Volpe happy and so we said our goodbyes.

Lorenzo opened the door to his car and made the gesture as if it was a chariot. For me, that FIAT was my chariot. It was exotic and different for this Jersey girl.

Before he closed the door, he made sure my seatbelt buckled. He leaned over to kiss my chest, then buried his head in my chest while his beautiful black curls bounced back and forth.

He moaned, "*Mi libellula bella* [my beautiful dragonfly] Ella, you make-a me crazy, mmm. Forget dinner, I want you so bad, *mi amore* [my love]."

I pulled his head from my chest and kissed him more passionately and deeper than ever before. If two people could have kissing sex, we were having it right now. I don't think there was any way for us to get any more into each other, literally.

After a few minutes, he pulled away and said, "Ok, we go eat or we never leave-a the parking lot."

We laughed, and I was so excited thinking about what the rest of the night could bring.

We went to the Eden Roc Hotel in Positano. They directed us to a table for two at the end of the balcony that was hidden in the vines hanging from the portico. It was a spectacular view of the mountains of Positano, with all the flickering lights reflecting on the water.

The way the table was situated, we were able to sit next to each other. Lorenzo was quite happy with this arrangement because he could look right down my top and have his hand travel up my legs at the same time.

He was on fire tonight. I don't know if I could have stopped tonight's magic if I tried, but why would I even try?

My strict Catholic upbringing was really being challenged, and I thought about the serious talk I had with Jesus a few hours earlier. I'm telling you right now, Jesus, that I won't be able to say, 'No' to him with my natural strength. If you want me to say, 'No' then you're going to have to intervene because I don't have the strength to turn this sweet boy down. Amen. Your favorite sinner." I made the sign of the cross.

I Need You Tonight

"Every time I hear this INXS song, it transports me right back to Italy and I imagine it always will." Lora Condon

The night felt so very special. I let Lorenzo lead with the ordering since we had the same taste in food. Of course, we started our meal with Prosecco. He ordered lobster with gazpacho and beef tartare. We also ordered chicken breast stuffed with pistachios, sea bass and capers.

The taste, the smell and most of all the memory of my grandmother putting capers in the Christmas Eve spaghetti aglio olio [garlic and oil] with anchovies brings me back to my favorite holiday meal.

Dinner was amazing, like almost every meal in Italy. The professional wait staff pays so much attention to detail. I didn't want to eat too much before dancing, so we didn't have dessert but we did have limoncello; there's always room for limoncello.

I loved the romantic dinner at this beautiful restaurant, and I didn't want it to end. I also couldn't wait to get out of there so I could wrap my arms around him, dance and kiss him with wild abandon. Leaving the restaurant, we walked all the way down the hill to the beach club and waited outside for Angela and Stella.

I was glowing from head to toe and I could see the other guys checking me out. My tan was on point, thanks to my newest and best friend, carrot-based Nivea. The juicy lip gloss with the red coral in a small bottle that the Cinque's put in my purse was shimmering to match the subtle shimmer in my dress.

It looked magical under the moonlight. I stole Enzo's secret and put some olive oil on my legs and tapped the excess on my cheekbones. My hair was half up and half down, with a few curls naturally falling around my face. My new dragonfly clip was helping to keep my hair big, high, and close to the heavens. I felt pretty. This was an unfamiliar feeling.

As we waited for the Volpe girls, almost about every person going into the club had to say, "Hello," to Enzo. I was so proud to be with him. Everyone loved him and so did I. A lot of the girls did a double take, because they were used to seeing me on the boat looking like a drowned rat with frizzy, wild hair. Tonight they realized why Lorenzo was so into me. He saw past the drowned rat and saw the princess.

Finally, the Volpe girls arrived, and we all went into the club together and decided on a time to meet back outside. Nothing happens in Italian clubs until later, so I knew this was going to be a long night and early morning. I expected to hear all Italian music but instead, they played a lot of American pop songs. We had the best time dancing. Unfortunately, I had to share him with Angela and Stella until their boyfriends arrived. Their boyfriends worked in the hotel and restaurant industry, so they worked late.

The DJ at the club was great. There was a great mix of Italian club music and American hits like Cyndi Lauper, Taylor Dayne and George LaMonde.

No Italian club is complete without some Eros Ramazzotti. One of my favorites is Taxi Story. It always reminds me of the song "Maniac", from *Flashdance*. Watching sexy Eros sing on the video screen at the club didn't hurt the party, either. I had to laugh when they played Jovanotti's song, "Gimmie Five". Hearing Italian rap was somewhat laughable, but it was fun and catchy.

After dancing for a while, Lorenzo grabbed my hand and led me out of the club. I asked him what we were doing, and he said, "Trust me." I was so nervous because I was pretty sure I knew what this meant.

Before leaving the beach club, he stopped to see his friend, and they went into his office for a few minutes. He came out with a bag of stuff and keys. We walked quickly to what I assumed was his friends Vespa, and he handed me the bag and said, "Hold on tight, baby."

"Where are we going?" I asked, as I hopped on behind him.

We drove a few minutes and ended up back at the San Pietro. I had no idea what he had in mind. We entered the hotel and completely blew by the front desk guy, who was looking down. We slid into the elevator that descended to the deserted beach cove.

Ok, now I know what's happening! The ride in the elevator was the longest ride ever. I was busting with anticipation. As we exited the elevator, it was almost pitch black, except for the moonlight and the lights from the wedding reception at the hotel. This little cove was magical. I could tell he was so proud of himself for thinking of this secluded spot.

As I was looking up at the moon, he stood in front of me and cupped my face in his hands. He told me he loved me and wanted to make the most of every minute we had together.

The summer was almost over and he couldn't bear the thought of not seeing me all the time. I reassured him we would see each other again; but really, I didn't know what the future held for either of us.

He looked me dead in the eye and with such a serious face, he said, "Mariella, I want you. I don't think I can wait. You are so beautiful and you're mine, and I want to give myself to you."

He was saying this as a statement, but also questioning if it was ok to make love. There would be no going back and forth with him trying to get in my pants like an octopus and me saying, "No," or him trying again in a few minutes and me saying, "No," again and again for an hour until I sent him home with blue balls. Inside myself, I laughed, because it was so darn cute and no Jersey guy would do this and be so sweet, and patient; basically asking permission to have sex.

This was what I was waiting for and my response was a big kiss on the lips and I pulled the belt loop on his pants to pull him into me. That was all the green light he needed, and he took over. In my head, I heard the woman's voice from Cinque's store, who told me to let him lead and I'll have the best summer of my life. I was excited to let Lorenzo lead me into this new chapter of my life.

Enzo spread one towel on the beach next to the large rocks in the cliff and propped me up on one rock that had a long, flat surface.

He was very careful to take out my dragonfly hair clip and place it on the towel. He loved to run his fingers through my curls and pull my hair when things got heated between us. Kisses started on my neck and slowly moved down my chest. As he moved down, he slowly unzipped the back of my dress, so I could barely feel it. Yes, he's a pro, I thought to myself. With my dress fully unzipped, he put his hands on my thighs and then slid them to my butt cheeks. He picked me up so my legs would wrap around his waist. Then he lifted my dress up over my head. He carefully dropped it on the towel so it wouldn't get dirty from the rocks.

This was driving me into such a frenzy I forgot I was even wearing anything, let alone this gorgeous, pure white lace dress. I was so dizzy with anticipation, I probably would have thrown the dress out to the Mediterranean had he not been so careful.

I had to grip his muscular shoulders and hold him tightly to not lose our balance as his one hand went down between his legs. Once inside, his face changed from a man on a mission to one filled with love, care and compassion, with an emphasis on passion. He was so concerned about me. This all felt completely natural and nothing was uncomfortable or awkward as I was led to believe by childhood rumors. I was grateful for his large frame and well-developed muscles to hold on to so I wouldn't fall. Ahh, I thought to myself, so this is what muscles are really for, not just pretty to look at.

Once we got situated, he placed me on the flat rock. We moved in sync with the waves crashing against the rocks. The sounds of the waves echoed throughout the cove, so it was almost impossible for anyone to hear us had anyone been there. As the waves and tide slowed down, we could hear the music from the hotel wedding.

The song that was playing was "I Need You Tonight" from INXS. We both noticed it at the same time, laughed and sang the chorus to each other for a few bars as we made love to the rhythm of the song.

This couldn't have been more perfect and beautiful. With my legs still wrapped around him, he shifted on top of me, breathed heavily, and kissed my neck and face.

I loved the way his curls were long enough to hit my cheeks, as he would bend down to kiss me. His hair was usually styled with his longer curls brushed back. When it got wet, humid or if I ran my fingers through it too much, the curls would come loose and he looked wild, free and incredibly sexy.

When he finally rested his head on my chest, our hearts were pounding in sync. He tapped his fingers on my chest mimicking our hearts beating together and said, "Even our hearts agree, we go together."

As I lie there, I felt like I was a new woman, or rather, an official woman. I could never go back to who I once was and nor would I. Everything seemed more vibrant and alive and I was more alive. I kept all of this to myself because I knew I was not his first. I'm pretty sure men don't feel like this after their first time. Even the ocean air smelled different and better than before. The moon was whiter than I had ever seen it before and everything seemed to be in Technicolor or Willy Wonka vision. His eyes were greener than I remembered and the blue specks were bluer.

Now I could see some amber flecks, sparkling right out of his eyes, into mine. I was privately having my own awakening to a world I never knew existed. I reveled in this feeling.

He reached over and opened the bottle of Prosecco. We were so thirsty we drank right from the bottle. It made me feel more primal, and I liked it. The bubbles felt like Pop Rocks in my mouth with every sip. I felt magical, even without my dress.

Without missing a beat, Enzo smiled at me, kissed my forehead, grabbed my hand and suggested we take a dip before we go back. He made it all seem so natural and nonchalant. It was like the circle of life under the Positano moon. The Mediterranean washed away the old Mariella to reveal the new, *libellula bella*, Mariella. The water was warm and calm, matching our energy.

We dried off and went back up to the elevator. We could hear everyone singing at the wedding. I couldn't understand what they were saying in Italian, but I knew it was Neapolitan by the way they were pronouncing the letter S. It's a heavy "sh" sound indicative of a Neapolitan accent or Napolidan as we say in America. Lorenzo told me it was "Scalinatella," sung by Roberto Murolo.

It was about a man chasing a girl on a narrow staircase in Positano that goes down near the Marina Grande beach right where we were headed toward the club. The staircase was actually near a Villa Tre Ville that was once owned by the famous Italian opera and film director, Franco Zeffirelli.

In true Italian dramatic fashion, the song is about a girl who left on a steamship and his love is now thrown into the ocean.

When we exited the elevator, someone from the wedding party knew Lorenzo and dragged us into the wedding; right up to the stage to sing and dance. One of my favorite songs, "Lazy Mary" by Lou Monte was playing. They were passing the microphone around and when it got to the English part; I happened to get the microphone. Well, when in Rome or Positano, sing!

So, I sang my best Lou Monte, and sang the English part. It's such a silly song telling lazy Mary to marry a fireman because she smokes in bed.

I had no idea what the English translation was for the last few lines that were in old Neopolian Italian except for the food in the last two verses. It's so much fun to sing and dance to. It's right out of The Godfather and made me feel like I was at my one of my family's weddings the way they used to be.

We laughed and danced for one more song, then we had to get going back to the club. Another song and I might have wanted to get married and really scare Enzo away. I was clueless as to the time, but I knew we had better get back ASAP. What a way to end the best night of my life.

We hopped on the Vespa and made it back to the club. The Volpe girls were standing outside on the beach with their boyfriends. Their eyes were burning a hole in my face, looking to see if "it" happened and if I was any different. I tried to keep a straight face, but I know I was blushing. I tried not to make too much eye contact with them. The girls said they were ready to go home, so we left. On the ride home, I told them about the wedding we crashed, hoping they wouldn't drill me with 20 questions upon our arrival.

Driving back to the villa was so peaceful. Everything was so dark and quiet. This little beach town rolls up when the sun sets. There are not too many lights other than the moon and a few lights by the docks.

I always loved the peace found by the docks at night. The dance between the fisherman's boats and the gentle waves is like a *"Tarantella"* [Italian wedding dance]. They come together and then move apart in one fluid motion.

We decided to go into the house through the boat room so we wouldn't wake up the Volpes. The girls went up so I could say goodbye to Enzo.

As I turned towards him, he grabbed me around my waist and pulled me into his chest. The moon gave us enough light to see each other's face, and he pushed me up against the wall with my head right next to the dragonfly tile. He kissed me so hard. His hands were now officially free to roam my whole body.

"Ok, loverboy, I have to get upstairs and you've had enough for one night," I joked. I half pushed him away, and he groaned.

"Never enough of my Mariella! Ok, I want to see you tomorrow and every day until you leave me forever."

"Don't say leave you forever, please." I almost cried hearing those words. We kissed again, and I said, *"Domani, mi amore,"* [tomorrow, my love] and winked goodbye. He slowly pulled himself away. Nodded his head, winked at me, and pursed his lips. God, he's so sexy. I am the luckiest girl in Italy.

Before I could get to the top of the first floor, Angela and Stella were waiting for me, making all kinds of kissy sounds and silly faces.

We ran into my room and they made me spill all the details. Thank God for them or else I would have burst with excitement and lost my mind. After dishing some juice, the sun started to rise.

We decided to finish the conversation tomorrow while we recovered on the docks. We weren't sure if rocking on the boats the next day would be the smartest idea after all that Prosecco.

Who knows? We're young, we can rally.

The next morning, we slept in and went to a late breakfast at Angelo's at the marina in Massa. Angelo's was my favorite place to eat breakfast, aside from our balcony. Breakfast is a great way to ease into the day and fantasize about what we're going to eat for our next meal. We got a plate of pastries for everyone to share.

The foam on their cappuccino was at an epic thickness this morning. I always wondered how they got their foam to be so thick. It barely came off the spoon when I tapped it on the side of the cup.

Angelo's is a great place to sit and look out at the boats while the fishermen bring in the day's catch for the restaurants. It doesn't get much fresher than this.

We decided to stay at the house, relax with the family and our boyfriends. We had a lazy day since we were all recovering from a late night. The Volpe's loved my story about crashing the wedding and singing "Lazy Mary" for everyone.

That's one of those magical memories that happens in Italy when you're not planning for anything to happen. We were so hungry and our cleaning lady offered to make us rabbit for lunch.

I wasn't sure about this since I raised rabbits as a kid, but I felt like I had to try it. The rabbit was so good, but I vowed to never eat it again. I just couldn't.

We listened to music all day, ate and slept in the sun. We had a lot of fun being together and singing. Thankfully, I was raised with enough classic Italian songs, I could sing with everyone. Mr. and Mrs. Volpe were musical encyclopedias, so I was getting a great education between them and Lorenzo. We sang to Sinatra, Louie Prima, Tony Bennett and, of course, Pavarotti.

There was this other very cute song called, "Ma La Notte,

No" [But The Night, No] by Renzo Arbore. It was a very catchy tune, but to try and figure out what he was saying didn't translate well.

Basically, the song says: "the day is hard, but the night, no". That became my new phrase to tease Lorenzo about not having sex at night. Lorenzo made sure it was *"ma la notte, si".*

Lorenzo had to work later in the afternoon, so we decided to meet after he was done. Thank God that his family covered some of his shifts so we could be together. Even his mother helped, which was very surprising. Then again, most Italian mothers have a hard time saying, "No," to their spoiled sons.

That night we ate in Massa again at the marina, across from Angelos. The restaurant was called *Funiculi, Funicula,* and this is where I developed a deep love for *gnocchi*. I never had *gnocchi* before and I was immediately upset that they were kept from me my whole life. How could my mother do this to me?

They served these little potato pillows in a mini crock pot with cheese melted over the top with *marinara,* or, as I called it, *marinad.* If you didn't know, you'd think it was French onion soup. This was way better. I also learned they are little lead bombs, and it's best to share them or plan on only eating that and nothing else. Thank God for the loose, flowing sundresses. It takes great skill to cook them so they do not get *mushad* or mushy.

I saw Lorenzo almost every day for the rest of the summer. It was hot; it was heavy, and it was almost over. We tried not to talk about my impending departure and agreed to take advantage of every opportunity to be alone and have fun. Isn't that what a summer love is supposed to be about? It was difficult to always keep it carefree and light, but we tried.

We also spent many hours staring at each other, trying to remember every curve of each other's face and the sound of each other's voice. We spent all of his free time together. He usually came to our villa, and the Volpes got to know him very well. We were family, and this was the happiest time of my life.

Quando, Quando, Quando

Many nights we would ponder how every day could seem like a lifetime and having joy beyond compare," and I miss those days." Lora Condon

The day finally came that we had to say goodbye. Lorenzo came over for breakfast and we went to Angelo's for my last serious foam cappuccino and ciambella. How am I supposed to go back to New Jersey and back to my oh-so-average life? I just spent a few months with some of the wealthiest people in the Sorrento area. I was surrounded by importers, exporters, hotel owners, store owners, restaurant owners, bankers, art dealers, as well as their families. This was an education of a lifetime that I could never learn in a book. I can see why my parents scraped their pennies together to be able to send me to Italy.

They believed that there was no better education than travel and authentic life experiences. This trip would give me something to talk about within different social circles for the rest of my life.

During my final breakfast at Angelo's, we went over so many fun, crazy and unforgettable experiences we shared over the summer. We laughed so hard we cried and then we cried so hard we laughed.

There was nothing better than sitting and watching the fishermen and the boats going in and out of the marina. It's a mesmerizing dance while they bring fish right to the restaurants to cook for patrons each night. We talked about going to our special cave along the shoreline to make love one last time. We hesitated because the sooner we got there, the sooner we would be over.

Eventually, we went to the cave. Normally, we would rip each other's clothes off, but this time, we lay on the blanket and held each other. It was surprising he was so sad and mostly wanted comfort. It's rare to see a guy be so emotional and only want to be held or hugged for a few moments.

I really liked him, but I never thought much more of him than a summer fling, even though he was the greatest summer fling in history. I had to keep it all in perspective as much as possible to prevent myself from missing him too much. I went to Italy with the intention of finding a fantastic summer romance, seeing all the tourist sights and eating well. Mission accomplished.

He was amazing and I couldn't wait to tell everyone about him. I was pretty sure I'd never see him again, and I was totally ok with that fact. I held him and tried to make a few jokes or rub his head like a baby to break the awkwardness.

After our last intense lovemaking session in the cave, we got dressed and headed back to the villa to have our last lunch with the Volpes. Everyone was so happy to see Enzo and we sang one last song in the living room before we left for the Naples airport.

We chose to sing, "Quando, Quando" [when, when] along with Sergio Franchi. I was well versed in this version since Sergio Franchi was one of my parent's favorite singers. The song is asking, "when will I see you again so you can be mine and don't make me wait." We had such a fun time singing and doing our best Sergio impressions. We finished the last chorus together, basically yelling, "*quando,*" Our sing-a-longs were some of my favorite times together as a family.

I know Lorenzo loved it as well because his family was much

more serious.

We were all going to miss Lorenzo, and he was going to miss all of us. We were together almost every day that summer, and I wondered what he would do once we left. I know I'd be crazy busy with college. His life would somewhat be the same once he went back to school. Would he have a line of girls waiting to take my place and would he even want them?

Now that I was an official woman, I was really picky about any future romances. What was another guy going to do for me or give me that Lorenzo hadn't already? There was no comparison. I got what I needed from my experience in Italy and then some.

Enzo said his goodbyes to everyone, and we all walked to the car to leave. When we hugged goodbye, he could barely speak. He was so upset. I felt so bad, but we both knew what we were getting into from the start. We promised to write, but I didn't think he would write too frequently. His life was fabulous and I'm sure his mother would have girls lined up so he would forget about me soon enough. The Nivea girl would be first in line for sure.

When Enzo opened the car door for me, the sunrays came through the trees right over the top of his head and created a halo effect. His eyes glistened from his tears and they became a deep green with amber lights coming out of them. He grabbed my wrist before I got in the car and turned my arm over. He drew an infinity sign on my inner arm and pointed to where my two hearts would have been like he did the day we first meet. He looked at me deeply into my eyes and said,

"Our hearts are-a forever tied together, you know-a this, yes?"

"Yes," I responded, "and I'm your *libellula bella L'americana*, Mariella."

We both laughed and ended on a happy note instead of a sad one. It was how I wanted to remember him and how I wanted him to remember us. Before he let go of my wrist, he took something out of his pocket and put it around my neck.

When I looked down, I saw it was a rosary made of wooden beads. I knew this was his favorite rosary, because Padre Pio held it in his hands and blessed it specifically for his family. I didn't want to take it because it is literally priceless, but he insisted. This relic gift meant more to me than anything. It was a blessing to receive it. I'm sure his mother would definitely not approve of this priceless gift being around my neck.

I got the best Italy had to offer, and I enjoyed every minute, loved every minute, and made the most of every minute as soon as my feet hit the ground. This was absolutely the best summer of my life.

Blessed Virgin of the Rosary

"The Rosary could very well be called the poem of human redemption." Blessed Bartolo Longo

On our way back to the airport, Mrs. Volpe wanted to stop at the Shrine of the Blessed Virgin of the Rosary of Pompeii. The church was restored by Bartolo Longo around 1875. Bartolo was so sad about the spiritual state of the people of Pompeii, he found a shrine that was in dreadful condition and decided to renovate it to its former glory. It's hard to imagine what it looked like based on the glorious basilica that stands there to this day. As Bartolo was raising funds to do the restoration, he received a beautiful and priceless painting of Our Lady of the Rosary from a convent in Naples.

During the restoration, miracles started happening and people started flocking to the shrine.

The church and Bartolo are special and unique. Bartolo was an Italian lawyer and at one time a satanic priest. After giving his life to satan he became more depressed, anxious and suicidal. Eventually, he renounced evil and was saved from satanic oppression. He became Catholic and even a Third Order Dominican. Bartolo then dedicated his life to the rosary and the Virgin Mary. On a side note, Domincans are named after St. Dominic who was given the rosary by Mother Mary when she would supernaturally visit him.

As we walked into the church, we stopped to take in the gorgeous gold leaf, frescos and priceless artwork. The sun shining through the stained glass windows was divine. Catholics sure do know how to make a church! You can't help but feel the power, glory, and vastness of God in a Catholic Church. The painting of Mary and the rosary did not disappoint either.

No one was in the church, so we were able to get as close as possible. We all stood looking at the painting, held hands, and prayed. We said a *Hail Mary* and an *Our Father*. When we all turned to leave, we noticed we were all crying and then we all started laughing. It was extremely powerful. If you've never stood under a magnificent sculpture or painting of Mary or Jesus, add it to your bucket list.

Stand in solitude and become one with the art. You don't even have to think about anything. Just feel. I'm guessing we weren't the only ones crying under this painting because there was a box of tissues on the pew behind us. Many felt the warm embrace of Mary and Jesus in that church.

After we went back out to the car, I had to go back inside and light a candle for my grandfather. I ran in and went right back to Mother Mary. I broke down and asked for forgiveness for being with Lorenzo. I couldn't resist him. I loved him and asked Mary to please make him my husband. I begged her to make everything right. I had no idea how much I loved him, and now it was all starting to hit me.

The thought of being with anyone else seemed impossible. I knelt down praying for what seemed like an eternity and then a peace and calm I can't describe came over me. I actually started giggling and I was literally thanking God that no one else was watching me cry and then audibly laugh.

After wiping away my tears, I lit a candle and slowly walked out of the church. Upon returning to the car, they asked me if I was ok.

I said I was and asked why they asked. They said I had a strange smile on my face, like I had a secret or something happened. I kept my secret to myself, clutched my wooden Padre Pio rosary beads Lorenzo gave me before I left and said, "I'm great and ready to go home."

Shop the rosaries I've made and other products at www.thebeautybuster.com

While writing this book during quarantine 2020, I discovered my love of the rosary.

Everyone seems to give me their old rosaries, but I never prayed them before. During the Covid-19 quarantine, I went on YouTube and learned how to pray the rosary. Many of my rosaries kept breaking because they are so delicate, so I decided to make my own with beads and paracord. Problem solved.

I make them and either give them away or sell them. The profit from every red, white and green Italian rosary goes directly to specific Italian businesses listed in this book affected by Covid-19. This is my way of helping my beautiful Italy that has given me so much. They're not factory made so every rosary is different, unique and from the heart. It's my way of spreading faith, hope and charity. Ave Maria!

Shop the rosaries I've made at www.thebeautybuster.com

Part 3

Back to America

"Ah, come back again as you were then, then when I gave you my heart. Ah, come back to me..." Bellini, Norma

Lorenzo and I wrote to each other almost every month. I didn't know what it would lead to, but I couldn't wait to get his letters. His life went back to normal. He never mentioned any girls, nor did I want to hear of any. I loved hearing about who was dating whom and the Amalfi coast gossip. I looked most forward to the town gossip letters. It felt like my secret life might not be so far away after all. He kept asking me to come back with the Volpes next summer.

I was pretty sure that wasn't going to happen because I had to work that summer for college money. What a feeling of defeat. Even though his family had money, his mother would not give him the money to bring me back to Italy. His parents considered him cheap and sometimes free labor.

They funded his lifestyle, but not his life. He also had to work at the store more since his brother secured an internship for the summer. Maybe this is better off. We can part on a good note with great memories.

Going back to school was almost impossible. Nothing was ever going to be as exciting as my last summer. I had to hunker down, find a job, save money for school and spend this year studying.

I only told a few of my best friends about Lorenzo and what really happened. The rest of the crowd got the Disney version, and that was fine with me. No one needed to know anything. It all sounded so unbelievable, anyway. The rich and famous of the Amalfi coast meant nothing to anyone at the Jersey shore.

No one would be impressed unless I was hanging out with Versace, Gucci or Armani. If I wasn't so busy, school would have been truly miserable. It was such a sharp contrast from the summer. Reality can be pretty harsh.

By the end of the last semester, I was gearing up for my summer job to make every penny possible for college. One day, I got a letter in the mail saying the college awarded me a journalism scholarship.

This meant I only needed to make a few thousand dollars that summer in order to pay the rest of tuition and some expenses. This incredible news meant I could use some of my summer cash to go to Italy again with the Volpes for at least a few weeks. I would only need to pay for my ticket and some food.

I knew between Lorenzo and the Volpe's, my food bill would be minimal. Immediately, I started writing to Enzo to let him know I was coming back to Italy this summer. I guess I should have asked the Volpes first, but I knew I always had an open invitation to stay with them. I'll sleep on the floor. I don't care. Italy here I come, *amore mio* [my love]. A few weeks later, I got a letter from Enzo with a check to go toward my flight.

Thank-you, Jesus. He's such a good man. I definitely needed that money. I should have saved my money, but you only live once and I got the Italy bug. Italy is like a drug that I can't detox from.

Part 4

2nd Summer on The Amalfi Coast

Sorrento Moon

I always look for the moon in the middle of the sea.

The Volpes were in Punta Massa for a few weeks before me, so I flew to Naples and took the train to Sorrento, where Lorenzo picked me up. I couldn't wait to see Enzo. I could barely believe I was seeing him again. I could only imagine how great this summer was going to be. It all happened so quickly we didn't have time to write too frequently to discuss our plans.

I knew we would get to spend a few weeks together and whatever happened, happened.

When I saw him at the train station, he looked like he was glowing under the Sorrento sun. He had sunflowers and a huge smile waiting for me. It was the best, eyes open kiss. It felt right, and I still fit perfectly in his arms.

I felt my cheeks get hot from being so excited and happy. It was as if everyone around us disappeared and we were in our own sunburst bubble. The overwhelming emotions took me by surprise. I was smiling so big and I couldn't stop. He was so happy to see me. We were giddy.

I couldn't wait to get some real Italian food in me. He took me to the cutest place called Residence L'incante Sorrento. We kept driving up and up the mountain.

I had no idea where we were going. I thought we would go to the Grand Marina in Sorrento, but I guess he had another surprise for me. Finally, we parked right up against a stonewall, Italian style on the side of a mountain.

That meant I had to climb over the clutch and get out of the driver's door. We walked over to what looked a little like a very large house in the mountains of Piano di Sorrento. We walked in the front door and he waved to the person at the desk before we went up a little stairway to the rooftop. There was a bottle of Prosecco and some appetizers up on the roof with a table and 2 chairs set up for us. It was quiet and relaxing, with a beautiful view of the mountains. He thinks of everything. We had a light lunch, which was about 10 different small plates of food. A typical Italian small lunch! We ate it all. I missed real food so much the last year.

He kept laughing at me, but I didn't care. I starved myself the last few weeks, so I could eat everything, guilt free. On the property, they grow whatever is in season for ultimate freshness. While eating, Lorenzo kept kissing me and grabbing my hand. We were both so happy to be together again. It was pure joy.

We were non-stop talking about everything that happened in our lives since last summer.

After lunch, we headed to Massa to see the Volpes. Enzo had not seen them since last summer, so it was going to be a sweet reunion. We entered the house and everyone was sitting in the livingroom. As we walked in, they were so excited to see Enzo. It was like I didn't exist. I couldn't even get mad. I totally understood.

There was another couple on the balcony, and they came in to introduce themselves. The woman was Margarita, and the man, Luciano. I had never seen Margarita before, but I knew Luciano was a banker in the Sorrento area. He was extremely wealthy and married, but not to Margarita. I later learned she was called, an Opportunist. It's a fancy word for a woman who sleeps with wealthy men in return for fabulous vacations, dinners, money, apartments and the opportunity to run in circles with the most wealthy and famous men around the world. She was supposed to stay with the Volpes for only two weeks, but now she was staying a few more weeks courtesy of Luciano.

He is paying for her to stay at the Volpe's villa because if he got a hotel room for a woman, people would talk. He could take her to one of his other apartments, but she couldn't stay there all the time.

I saw the look of surprise on Lorenzo's face when Luciano turned around on the balcony and started walking towards us. Enzo played it cool and acted as if he didn't know what was really going on; but he did. Margarita was not anything special.

She was average looking and unassuming, which is why she was the perfect opportunist. No one suspects rich men to be running after her. She made her money because she was smart, kept her mouth shut, and didn't want to marry any of them or have their baby. She was safe and wasn't looking to be an all-out home wrecker. In her mind, she was providing a service.

These men were going to cheat no matter what, so they might as well do it with someone that will keep it all private. The men would never dare tell on each other. They kept quiet due to Man Code. Most of these men probably kept quiet because they knew they might eventually cheat as well.

We left the awkwardness and went to my room, unpacked and then hung out with the Volpes and their new guests. Family time meant music time and also my favorite time.

We had the standards from Sinatra, Pavarotti, and Jerry Vale, who was my grandmother's favorite. She was always singing, "I Can't Get You Out of My Heart" to my grandfather. Later we took a Prosecco break from singing and then finished with Mario Lanza's version of "Arrivederci Roma" from the 1957 film, *Seven*

Hills of Rome and Tina Arena's song, "Sorrento Moon", which became my new theme song for the summer. Both songs have a certain sadness about them.

Thinking of leaving Italy while singing "Arrivederci Roma", considering I just arrived, was too much for me to handle right now. I poured another glass of Prosecco.

"Sorrento Moon" is a beautiful song. There are not too many modern songs about Italy, so this song is special. We would play this over and over and sing it to each other under the Sorrento moon. Every time I hear this song, it brings me right back to Sorrento. I felt like some of the lyrics were written for us because the singer talks about waiting a long time to feel like she's in paradise with her lover under the Sorrento Moon.

Everyone was tired from the heat, and I was extra tired from the travel. We all decided to relax and then get ready for dinner in Sorrento. Lorenzo and I headed to our cove to make love and catch up.

I couldn't wait to be with him. He felt perfect and my body needed and missed him since I haven't been with anyone else since last summer. I didn't plan on not kissing another boy, but no one interested me. I was spoiled and now I had much higher standards.

No other guys could even come close to Lorenzo, and nothing even caught my eye. They all seemed like stupid boys. Lorenzo was a real man, as far as I was concerned.

I began to wonder if this was love and not just a summer fling. Everyone had made light of our romance. I'm not experienced in matters of love, romance, flings or marriage, but this seemed very real and very good.

It felt like a genuine relationship, not a summer romance. I'm not sure how I ever thought I could just forget all of this and him so easily after returning home.

Lying on his chest in the cave and listening to the waves crashing was so soothing. It put us both into a deep sleep. I desperately needed rest after the whirlwind of the last month. Now, I have peace. We watched the sunset from the cave and walked back to the house under the sweet Sorrento moon.

The Volpes surprised me with dinner at La Lanterna. Everyone, including the restaurant staff, was so happy to see Lorenzo and me back together. I always had so much fun going out with the Volpes. I loved greeting the staff at the restaurant. Italian greetings are the best by far. They make you feel famous and like you're the most special person in the world.

They all knew me well. Little fried fish, pizza, red wine, and *caprese* [mozzarella, basil and tomato] were my favorite dishes here. They also brought out a fish encased and cooked in a salt casket. They broke the casket with a hammer and the most wonderful, moist fish was sitting like a pearl in the center of an oyster.

This was the coolest dish, and the fish was divine. One would think that the fish would be too salty, but it was not. The salt casket makes the fish more moist and full of flavor.

We ate, we drank, we conquered. When dessert arrived, so did Lorenzo's family. It was nice to see them and a smart way to break the ice.

His mother gave me and my unfortunate choice of American clothing the once over. The remainder of his family was very excited to see me. Enzo's father was all smiles, hugs and cheek pinches.

His mother actually brought me a beautifully wrapped fragrance from the shop. I was hoping this was her way of showing us she was giving our relationship her blessing. Whatever it was, I'll take it. I only wanted good vibes while I was on vacation.

Dessert arrived, and it did not disappoint. We had *babas* and *torta Sorrento.* The *babas* were made so well, I wanted to take an extra plate home. *Babas* are cakes drenched in rum-spiked citrus syrup. Need I say more? The *torta* was warm, rich, dense and came with a side of vanilla ice cream. Espresso and of course, his homemade limoncello topped it all off. No cold stares from his mother could ruin my state of happiness.

God, I miss this food more than anything. I have been to some of the best Italian restaurants living in the New York area, but absolutely nothing compares to the food in Italy. Any Italian *nonna* [grandmother] can out-cook the best chefs in America. Italy is blessed.

It was good for our families to eat and spend some time together. Anything that would make Enzo's mother feel comfortable or happy for her son would make our relationship that much better.

I was hoping this was a turning point, but it was also the beginning of my trip. Everything went well, so I wasn't trying to make myself crazy wondering about her opinions. Right now, all I cared about was Enzo and his opinion of me. From what I could tell, everything between us was fantastic.

I didn't even care what or who he did when I was gone. I'm here now and that's all that matters. We said our goodbyes to his parents after dessert and then we rolled out into Tasso Square to take a walk before going back to the villa. It was hard saying goodnight to Lorenzo, but I had to get some sleep to prepare for more fun tomorrow.

The next morning, the Volpe girls and I got an early start boating with all their friends and Lorenzo. We used kayaks stored on the boats so we could go in and out of caves, grottos and hit up other beaches along the coast. Much to my surprise, there were some interesting developments in the relationship department.

Major drama. When we got on Angelo's boat, I noticed a girl with stringy, over-processed blonde hair and heavy, black kohl-lined eyes was smacking Angelo's butt as he was trying to drive the boat.

I looked at Enzo and my eyes got huge. I couldn't help but make a funny face. It was Marta with a little baby bump; I was in shock. She got pregnant, and they recently got married; I couldn't believe it.

So he did lead her on! God knows what else he did to this poor girl. Lorenzo informed me that I shouldn't feel too bad for her because now she has his money and baby forever. His family bought her a cheap tourist trinket store to run, so she would appear respectable.

She could also be self-sufficient if the marriage ever dissolved, which it rarely does in southern Italy.

Many rich men can cheat and remain married. It's cheaper to keep her, I guess. Everyone used to make fun of Marta, but she got the last laugh.

Angelo seemed to tolerate her and it seemed to be more of a sexual relationship rather than one of deep, mature love and respect. What judgments can we really make, though? The goal for her was marriage, a baby, and security. She got it all. Well played Marta, well played.

We kayaked into one of the coves and saw Giovanni and Giovanna also kayaking through the dark, secluded cave. This was our first meeting since last summer and Giovanna was so excited to show me her engagement ring that she almost flipped her kayak.

I felt like I missed so much over the last year. I was happy for everyone, but I also felt left out of sharing in our friends' lives. Enzo saw a touch of sadness on my face, so he stood up in our kayak and started singing.

He sang "Santa Lucia" in Neapolitan. It was sexy as hell and I hung on to every word. It was fitting since the song is mostly about being on a boat in the beautiful, breezy Bay of Naples with the incredible Saint Lucy, who also happened to be the patron saint of virgins.

This song is supposed to be the first song translated from Neapolitan into Italian. Lorenzo chose the original Neapolitan and I couldn't agree more. Enzo pretended he was my private gondolier while singing his heart out in a typical, passionate Italian style.

His voice echoed in the cave and sounded like a professional singer. My father and Mario Lanza, the man who made this song even more famous in 1959, would have been proud.

We spent our days boating, eating, hiking, shopping, and making love. We spent our nights eating, singing and hanging out in Vico Equense with his friends and, of course, making love anywhere and everywhere. We had sex outside all over the Sorrento Peninsula. I don't think we ever had sex on a bed. Welcome to sex Italian style. Lorenzo's family filled in for him at the store many days and nights so we could be together. I tried to duck his mother at any cost, and Lorenzo didn't push the situation.

We had no idea what was going to happen after this summer. I would go back to college and have to work. He would soon finish university and start his architecture career while still helping with the perfume store. Logistically and realistically, this would be our last summer with freedom. We never talked about the future or the reality of the situation.

We only tried to enjoy every minute and be present in the moment, which Italians have mastered.

Since I did not know when I would return to Italy, I stocked up on some of my favorite things at Vizi & Sfizi in Sorrento. Vizi & Sfizi is a gourmet food and cooking store that had many items I could bring back on the plane with me and give as gifts. I filled a basket with little sachets of raisins and orange peel chunks wrapped in olive leaves.

They were the perfect gift snacks to remind me of Sorrento. I got about 30 of them and I know the lady thought I was crazy. I tried to take a picture of the sign describing what they were, and the Gestapo saleslady almost ripped my camera out of my hand. She was yelling that I couldn't take any pictures in the store.

As she kept following me around, I saw Lorenzo snap some photos for me so I would know what the heck these amazing little things were. We had a few good laughs over that episode. I secured a few bottles of wine and local olive oil, along with a few bottles of orange marmalade, lemon soaps, black salt and fruit jelly. These are the little things you really miss once you no longer have access to them. I made sure to show Lorenzo what I liked and hoped he would mail me a care package before he forgot me forever. It was worth a try.

One night we were on his Vespa going to the town square in Vico Equense to hang out with his brother and friends. They were all standing up against a wall and I saw the Nivea girl dancing and staggering around the guys. When Enzo saw her, he made a turn up the mountain in a different direction. I asked him what he was doing, and he threw his hand up in the air. Oh boy, I know this means he's up to something.

We went around some winding roads and came up to a fenced in area. He slowed down and got off his Vespa to unlock the chain around the fence. I looked at him because he was acting like we were almost trespassing, but he obviously wasn't because he had the key. We drove through the entrance and it was the most spectacular lemon grove.

The smell was intoxicating. It was hot and humid the whole day and the thought of fresh lemons cooled me off. I asked him where we were and he sarcastically responded, "A lemon grove."

"Obviously," I said, but what are we doing here?"

He grabbed me, lifted me up and put me on the hood of a FIAT that was parked inside the grove. He laid on top of me and started kissing me and unzipping my pants.

I was a bit overwhelmed and said, "Um, Lorenzo, where are we? Whose lemon grove is this and whose car is this? Are we allowed to be here?"

"No problemma, Ella. This is the grove of *la mia famiglia* [my family]. No one is here."

Well, ok, I guess that's all the information I need right now; I thought to myself. So here I am on the hood of a FIAT, making love in a lemon grove on the side of a mountain in Italy. Did I mention I now have a whole new appreciation for FIATs?

In less than 10 minutes, we were both totally naked when we suddenly heard the chain lock rattling on the fence. We both froze, looked at each other and he had put his hand over my mouth because I was laughing with nervousness at being caught. I couldn't stop.

While he was still inside me, he yelled out, asking who was unlocking the lock. It turned out it was his brother. None of us were supposed to be there, yet here we all were. They were speaking Italian so quickly, I couldn't catch everything they said, but I heard his brother laughing and then drove away.

From what I could understand, his brother had a girl in his car and had the same intentions in mind. Lorenzo laughed in relief and went right back to what he brought me here to do. A few minutes later, Lorenzo abruptly stopped and reached down to the ground, picked up a lemon, ripped it in half and drizzled the lemon juice over my breasts. I asked him if he liked lemon that much, to which he responded,

"Yes, I love it."

Next thing I knew, he licked the cool lemon juice off my warm body. The difference in temperature between the lemon juice and my hot skin drove me wild. After we finished, we sucked on some of the lemon to refresh ourselves and drove back to the town center. His brother wasn't there, thank God. It's not like we were hiding anything, but I wasn't wanting his brother to see me in a lemon juice afterglow.

Back in the town square, Eros Ramazotti was blaring. I hadn't heard Eros since last summer and I missed seeing his gorgeous face all over the billboards. Unfortunately, he doesn't get any play on America radio. One of my favorite songs by Eros is, "Musica E' " [Music is]. I love this song because even if you don't know what he's saying, you can feel the passion.

The saxophone playing is great. The song is slow so I could actually hear the words and translate some of them and Lorenzo helped me with the rest. Of course, it's an emotional and passionate song, just like Italians.

The lyrics don't always translate well into English but they always make me smile. "Musica E'," talks about getting lost in the music and it's your friend who comforts you when you are lonely.

Postiglione

"I had no idea my love for ravioli could actually be genetic." - Lora Condon

During this trip, I had to go to the town where my family was originally from or else I would never hear the end of it from my mother. The town where we're from is called Postiglione, up in the Alburni Mountains of southern Italy. I had family there that I never met and a few cousins that visited us in New Jersey. They were cool, and it was pretty amazing how when they came to stay with us, they fit right in with the family. It was as if we grew up together. I barely spoke Italian, and they spoke some English.

My mother remembers a lot of her Italian, so we made it work when they visited. With enough food and wine, Italians can get along with anyone. Mr. Volpe made sure I got there to visit, so he didn't have to hear my mother nag him for another year.

We drove up the winding roads to the top of the mountain. We met with my cousins who owned the same chestnut farm that my great-grandfather owned and they even lived in the house he owned. It was like stepping into a time warp with a town population of only 2,000. One of the most spectacular things about this town is that you feel you could reach up and touch the clouds. I was expecting Alberto Tomba, La Bomba, to come skiing down the side of the mountain any minute with that big, beautiful smile on his face.

The town dentist, Donato came out to greet us and as it turns out, he had done some research on my family tree and knew all about some of our relatives. He made sure we got the full tour of the town. He had the same nose as my grandmother and it made me wish my family had never left Italy. They all felt like family and I'm forever grateful.

The middle of town had a huge tree. If you look out over into the ocean from that tree, you can see Capri and Vesuvio. What a view! We met with my cousins and walked through town to get a cappuccino because Americans always want a cappuccino no matter the time of day, much to Italian's chagrin. As we walked around, they showed me a Padre Pio statue right in front of a church. I wondered why a Padre Pio statue would be here, and they told me that the other priest in the statue was Padre Clemente Tomay from Postiglione. He was Pio's confessor and friend.

Man, I wish my mother was here right now. On at least two occasions, Clemente said he smelled Padre Pio's holy perfume, which is said to smell like violets. That smell was indicative of his stigmata. A very strong, beautiful, violet fragrance would surround Padre Pio and many people would smell it when his presence was near them, even if he wasn't there physically. I almost felt like Padre Pio was following me or calling me. Part of me thought I was out of my mind and the other part felt like maybe this was some typical supernatural Catholic stuff. Whatever it was, I made a mental check.

We slowly walked back to the town center and it was like an eating tour. Growing along the sidewalks and roads were wild *finocchio* [fennel] or fanuke as we call it. We ate wild rosemary, apples, chestnuts and basil. This town was an open juicy buffet. Once we reached the town center, we went to one of the popular restaurants, La Doga. Since my cousins knew everyone, the owner let us go back into the kitchen to watch the old *nonna* [grandmother] make homemade pasta.

She and the other women were masters at their craft. They formed the pasta to create all different shapes and sizes. Michelangelo had nothing on these ladies. They made the pasta so fast and had perfected each shape with the precision of any modern machine. They took little pasta balls and rolled them along a piece of wood with grooves in it, only using their thumb to reveal a perfect spiral. I gave it a shot and only made a mess. My pasta had no swirl, just a lump with a dent!

We stood there amazed and in awe of these women. Once again, people had a good laugh at L'americana.

Thankfully, the restaurant had pasta already made, so we didn't have to eat my lumps. We ordered a bunch of dishes to share and when the ravioli was passed to me; I jokingly took the whole dish of ravioli for myself because I love ravioli so much. Ravioli is one of my all-time favorite foods. Growing up, we even had a cat that loved ravioli. Surprisingly, they informed me that ravioli is the dish Postiglione is known for making the best. I knew there was a reason why I loved ravioli so much. It's amazing how strong genetics can be. The food didn't stop coming, especially because this was my first trip to Postiglione and they were so proud of their town, heritage, history and the fact that I came back to see where my great-grandfather lived. Of course, the wine was tremendous, and it actually came right from a winery down the road. Wow, this town gets better and better.

I can understand why my great-grandfather came back to live in his hometown after 20 years in America. This place is heaven. I can only imagine him landing in Newark, New Jersey and thinking to himself he should turn tight around and get on the boat back to Naples.

After lunch, we drove a few minutes to Tenuta Macellaro, the town winery. It was charming. We drove up the unpaved road to the winery, and once we got up the hill, it was like magical miles of vineyard.

The owner, Ciro Macellaro and his stunningly beautiful wife came out to greet us because they were so happy to have guests. I already had a tasting at the restaurant but I was looking for more tastings and more importantly, buying. Once they found out that we already had their wine and loved it so much that we had to come visit, they were overjoyed.

When found out my family was originally from their town, they went into royalty mode. All the family came out to greet us and to see who this crazy American was that came almost 2 hours from Sorrento to see her family's town. I already love them like family.

We enjoyed more amazing reds and one in particular, called *Panormo*, named after the mountains. It knocked me out, so I called it the Rocky Marciano wine. I left with a few bottles to shove into my suitcase, but not nearly enough. I also couldn't leave without the rose'.

It was the opposite end of the red, but still so crisp and refreshing. The owners are artists, not just vintners. With each sip, the owners would smell, swirl, sip and enjoy every sensation of their very own creation. It was fascinating to watch.

Before we left, the owners showed us their olive oil production. Lorenzo automatically put some olive oil on his lips and smacked them together. He took the extra from his fingers and put it around his eyes. "My mother's secret for her beautiful skin," he said.

"Give me a bottle, please. Actually, make it two," I joked to the owner.

We all needed to walk around and work off some of the food and wine. My cousins and I went to the cutest little strawberry farm where they make luxury strawberry liquor. Fragolino Milles uses the sweetest, tiny strawberries to create a beautiful *aperitivo* [pre-meal drink] to drink alone or have with Prosecco.

These tiny strawberries pack one heck of a flavor punch. We did enjoy it both ways and then bought some to share with everyone back home. This was something new, so I knew they'd all love it.

The next day, we did some hiking around town. Everywhere you go in that town is a hike because it's basically one big mountain. At the top of the town is the Normanno Castle, which was built to protect them from the Turks and any other potential invaders. It was pretty much abandoned, but the grounds were well-kept and it had great panoramic views of the whole town below. I kept thinking this would make a great spa or retreat home or monastery. Maybe Lorenzo and I would get married right on the grounds of this castle overlooking my great-grandfather's home.

My mind was racing, thinking of all the possibilities. I had to stop myself because I knew I wasn't even supposed to be here this summer, let alone fantasize about getting married here!

After the castle, we got to see my great-grandfather's home and even went inside. It was so cute and all I could do was imagine my ancestors living in this house and hiking the hills every day, and how shocking it must have been to land on Ellis Island.

My cousins told us all about our family history and how we are supposedly related to Tony Mottola, the guitar player. Tony was famous for "the Danger chord," which was a dissonant chord used for building tension in scary scenes of the movie Danger. Tony was a true Jersey boy and also one of Frank Sinatra's favorite guitar players. I knew about this, but I could never figure out how we were related.

My great-grandfather had two families, and we got split, but my grandmother always said we were all related. I tried many times to get a hold of Tony's relative, Tommy after Tony died, but it's almost impossible to get a hold of such a big celebrity. It would be awesome if we had a family reunion in Postiglione, Italy!

My family went from Postiglione, Italy to Kearny and Newark, NJ, and then back to Postiglione. I had always hoped I would be a part of such a cool, family history. One day, I hope to find out if we're truly related.

It was such a special two days with family and new friends. I never felt more connected to Italy and my family. What a gift. I'm so glad my mother made me go visit Postiglione, I finally found my people and I'll never look at a ravioli the same way again.

Rethinking My Life Plan

"All the things we wanna be, let's run away to Italy." Lisa Rowe

As much as I loved the mountains, I needed the ocean and was glad to get back to the coast. I needed to see the blue sea moving and alive with love and life. The ride back to the villa gave us plenty of time to sing with the radio. I was basically in charge of the radio, as his free hand was always on the clutch or my leg, driving both of us crazy. We liked the same music and it also gave me an opportunity to learn some new Italian songs. I think a lot of the new songs are kinda cheesy, but they're fun and light, like the Italians.

The coastal road before you get into Sorrento always reminds me of Matt Monro's song from the movie, *The Italian Job*. "On Days Like These". It was written in 1969 and it still fits this drive perfectly. We opened the windows and let our crazy, curly hair flow with the wind. There are not too many things that can make one feel so free, wild and pure, like the wind blowing through your hair, music jamming and cruising around the mountain.

When we got back to Massa, one of the Volpe's friends was out on the jetties, making out with what appeared to be the Speedo twins. Francesco and Federico were twins given that nickname due to them wearing the skimpiest Speedos. We watched; we had to watch.

We couldn't believe it was happening, but it was and right before our eyes. I knew those rocks very well, and I knew they were doing it to entice everyone on the coast. There was only one spot on those rocks that was secluded from the coast, and it definitely was not there.

This lady was married to one of the biggest hotel moguls in the area, and I couldn't believe she would leave herself exposed like that in more ways than one. As we watched and giggled, the three of them drifted into the section of the jetty that was hidden from the coast and only God knows what happened after that.

When she came back to the coastline, she was by herself and she ran right into the arms of her husband, who showed up to have drinks with the Volpes. Lorenzo and I were uncharacteristically quiet during happy hour and she kept asking if we were ok. We didn't know if she knew we saw them or not, but she definitely knew that we would have been able to easily see her from where we were sitting.

To buy our silence, she invited all of us to dinner at a gorgeous hotel in Sorrento called Imperial Hotel Tramontana. If she's buying, I'm eating and I have the perfect dress. I've been wanting to pull out some of my Cinque dresses, anyway. Clothes are the quickest way for a girl to feel fabulous and this was the place to look fabulous for sure. When she mentioned this hotel, I saw Lorenzo's eyebrow rise a bit. He knew we were being bought and so did I but I definitely didn't care. Me not accepting dinner wouldn't stop her from cheating. Her husband is probably doing the same thing, like many of the very wealthy men in this area. Her secret was safe with us. I'm just a guest and not looking to rock any boats here. Enzo was more of a live-and-let-live kind of guy. He has seen it all and lets people fall on their own sword.

Off to the Imperial Hotel Tramontano, we went. I was so excited because I'd heard so much about it. Upon entering, I literally stopped and had to take it all in. Enzo didn't expect me to stop, so he kept going and almost ripped my arm off. He turned back, started to say something when he saw a look on my face he never saw before; I was in awe. The colors. The marble.

The beauty and art. I don't know how to explain it, but I wanted to melt into the walls and marble. The décor was the typically spectacular neon lemon yellow, Mediterranean blue, the greenest of plants, and life-changing views of the Gulf of Naples. I never want to leave Italy. Every corner is filled with breathtaking beauty that makes me wonder why on earth I would ever leave.

This hotel was making me rethink my whole life plan. Did I even want to go back to America? Was being rich or successful in New York that important or was being able to enjoy this view whenever I want, the true meaning of life? Never did I think a hotel would make me rethink my whole life, but here I am.

Lorenzo went to pull me ahead, but I pulled him back toward me. "Lorenzo, I never want to leave here. I'm serious," I said, almost in tears. His silence told me he didn't know what to say. I was too young to move across the globe. My mother would kill me and I'm not fluent in Italian; yet!

He put his arm around me and we took it all in. I could feel the history and had to ask him about this gorgeous establishment. He promised to tell me later. We joined our group, and I felt stupid because I was the only one in awe of this beauty; they are used to seeing it.

This was nothing special for them. I prayed I would never be bored with this view. The owners came over and I asked them about the history of the hotel. I wanted to know everything. The owner was so excited to share his passion for the hotel with a young American girl.

The very terrace we were sitting on is where the song, "Torna A Surriento" [Return to Sorrento] was written. I can totally see the inspiration. This was someone's actual home until 1812, before they turned it into a hotel. Writers like Milton stayed here for an extended period of time, and Harriet Beecher Stowe was so inspired, she wrote, *Agnes of Sorrento,* right here. James Fenimore Cooper also lived here while finishing, *Water Witch.* The coolest part was that the poet Torquato Tasso was born here. Considering Tasso Square is the exact place I fell in love with Italy, this hotel had a special place in my heart.

Many of the royals throughout history have walked through these doors, enjoyed the same view and potentially used the same exact fork. I was in my geek glory. The owner had to go back to work, because I was taking up way too much of his time. I didn't even know some of the names he rattled off, but I'm sure they were important. It's pretty safe to say, he's not going to be telling any future guests that Mariella Pecoraro, ate right at this very table.

To work off all this good food, we decided that tomorrow we would hike The Path of the Gods. I didn't know how difficult this hike would be, but everyone assured me it would definitely burn off some calories. When we met up with the guide, I immediately recognized him as Nino Aversa from Sorrento Hiking.

He's the world-famous guide I saw on Italian T.V., always with a happy face. We knew him as an expert on the Sorrento Peninsula, and in true Lorenzo fashion, he got us the best tour guide to make a magical experience for me. He even had a little dragonfly clipped to his backpack. It was a good sign. The hike is breathtaking, and with every step, I wanted to take a picture. The views span from Capri to part of the Amalfi Coast. This excursion was a few hours but felt like it was flying by quickly.

This trek makes you feel like you are seeing the real Italy. Although there are no big tourist attractions, the real attraction is the beauty of the country. You'll see cliffs, the bluest ocean and sky followed by the smell of wildflowers. Along the trek, we stopped at a goat herder's rest area and Nino set up lunch for us.

We had some wine, cheese and meats, all handmade by the goat herder. This was a once-in-a-lifetime experience and off the beaten path for sure. Everything was fresh and welcomed after hiking on a hot day. I figured we burned off enough calories from last night, so we could indulge this afternoon.

I loved hearing the bells on the goats. They're so happy and free. I felt transported back in time. Lunch was charming and watching the goats graze was mesmerizing. I could see why they considered Nino the best guide on the Amalfi Coast.

He had other tours, and we immediately jumped at the chance to go on the pasta and limoncello tour. Even Lorenzo learned some more history. I loved doing some different activities since I spent most of my time boating and not touring.

As my time in Italy was drawing to an end, Lorenzo and I spent almost every day together because we knew this was going to be the end. His mother even felt pressured to have me over at their house for dinner to show she was playing nice or maybe she was having dinner to send me off forever. She was warming up to me; I hoped. Nervously, I tried to find the right outfit. I don't know why I cared, because I was pretty sure I'd never see Enzo again, but I did it for him. I pretended to be hopeful for him and I pretended to enjoy spending time with his mother. I hoped she didn't put the *malocchio* [evil eye] on me. I subconsciously grabbed my corno.

He picked me up for one of my last rides on his Vespa to take me to his home. It was bittersweet. Their home was beautiful and had a view of the ocean with a gorgeous breeze that went through the entire house. It was a stunning home and everything was perfect, like a museum. I think they even had a fragrance piped throughout the home. We had appetizers on the balcony and then moved into the formal dining room for the main meal.

Everything was perfect, formal, and cold. I was pretty sure there would be absolutely no singing and dancing in the living room tonight. Dinner consisted of pleasant conversation about school, work, family, and the weather. I kept smiling at Lorenzo and wondered if he was thinking about how different our families act.

His brother and sister were more quiet than normal as well. His mother was an excellent cook and made *cacio e pepe* [spaghetti with cheese and pepper]. Enzo obviously told her this was one of my favorite dishes, so she made it for me.

I was very honored, and I truly appreciated the kind gesture. Raving about the food took up at least another five minutes before more uncomfortable silence. It was a nice evening, but the elephant in the room was me living in America and her son living in Italy. One of us had to move or forget all about each other.

Her eyes did not hide her disapproval of our relationship. I blew it off because I had no idea what was going to happen in the future. Realistically, I figured I'd find my true love while writing for Rolling Stone or Billboard Magazine. I would have a fabulous New York City life that people only dream about while being the first to write about the hottest spots in the city.

After dinner, we left and headed back to the lemon grove. I knew exactly where he was taking me and I was ready for a different taste of lemon heaven.

He brought a blanket, pillows and limoncello to go with the atmosphere. I wanted to spend time with him because I was pretty sure this would be our last time together forever. I couldn't see how I could afford to go to Italy and his mother would never allow him to come to America to see me. She was too afraid he'd never come home.

As soon as we entered the gate, I got butterflies. It felt like the first time all over again. I figured since we have lemons, we should make limoncello. We sat down on the blanket, had some limoncello, and talked about how amazing it was to spend another summer together. We briefly touched on our plans for school, but it was too painful to talk about our impending separation. The truth was evident, and there was no denying it.

Not wanting to waste the last of the limoncello, he poured it over my chest and licked it off. He then dripped it straight down my stomach and inched my pants off as he dripped the limoncello. He was in no rush for this night to end, and neither was I.

He made sure to leave enough limoncello for my whole body. He was savoring every lick and taste. I couldn't have been more happy, more relaxed and in any more ecstasy. He was memorizing my body and every inch of me to last a lifetime. I loved everything about him.

His massive hand could hold both my breasts at once and his other hand could almost cup my whole bottom. Maybe it would have fit at the beginning of the summer, but I was totally overloading on carbs with reckless abandon. I'm pretty sure he didn't notice and he definitely never complained. By the time we were done, we were literally sticking to each other from the sugar.

He got the hose from the farmhouse and with the greatest care; he made sure he rinsed every inch of my body off and smooth. I returned the favor. We drank, talked, and made love over and over until we were exhausted. Slowly, we walked back to the car to return to the villa.

To think this was the end of us was devastating. We totally rocked the Amalfi Coast. We were "an item" and "a thing" and everyone was jealous of our love.

We couldn't bear to part ways, so I snuck him back to my bedroom at the Volpe's villa. I slept in his arms, under the Sorrento moon wrapped up by the sweet breeze from the Bay of Naples. He sang me to sleep with Louis Prima's, "Buona Notte." I love everything Louis Prima and think he was one of the greatest American musicians and a pure entertainer. Anyone who can fit the word "bacala" into a song and make it work is a genius in my book. You. can see David Lee Roth took so much of his "jump jive" from him.

We sang to him so often that Lorenzo knew all the words even though he never heard of him before. Before I drifted off to sleep Lorenzo sang the sweet words from the song Buona Sera. All I remember is hearing something about a wedding ring on my finger and I love you. That was all I needed to hear.

I had to leave early the next morning. Since Mr. Volpe had to go to Naples for some business, he took me to the airport while Lorenzo had to go to work. This parting was different for me than the last time.

I had a deep, hurting pit in my stomach. These past few weeks were a gift, and I knew this was going to be the end. I left a huge part of my heart in Italy. I distracted myself well enough last year, so I didn't feel the pain so much, but this year, it was almost impossible to control my feelings. This was a pain I've never felt before and hoped to never feel again.

Who could ever live up to Lorenzo? I'm afraid this will be the highlight of my life and I'm too young to say that. Lorenzo and I said very little before I left. We hugged so tightly and promised to write; but for what purpose? I thought to myself, I'll never see him again.

I couldn't bear to think logically or about the future. Couldn't we pretend it wasn't goodbye forever, but until next summer? We tell ourselves all kinds of lies to get through life and this would be my biggest lie to myself.

Mr. Volpe and I said very little on the road to Naples. He knew that coming to Italy next year would be almost impossible.

He also knew that Lorenzo's mother would never bankroll his trip to America to see me. Summer is the busiest time for his store and the only time I could actually get away. His uncharacteristic silence reinforced my impending doom.

To soften the blow, Mr. Volpe stopped in a supermarket and bought me a few bottles of Villa Massa, Limoncello, the one we often drank at the house. Once I boarded the plane, I put on my headphones and played one of my favorite songs, "Core 'ngrato" and tried to sleep the entire flight home.

Part 5

Il Postino

"Poetry doesn't belong to those who write it; it belongs to those who need it." Il Postino

After months of writing to Lorenzo with no response, I finally received a letter on a gloomy Saturday. I was so excited I ripped open the letter to read that he was so sorry he hadn't written because he thought I stopped writing him. He recently learned his mother was taking my letters and throwing them in the garbage as soon as they arrived at their perfume store to where I was writing. Since his schedule changed with school, his mother was now at the store when the mail arrived.

She was so worried he would move to America she threw my letters away for the last few months. I was shocked. He gave me another address at his friend's store and said to mail everything there. So that's what we did. I can't say it made me feel confident that I would ever see Lorenzo again in Italy or America.

His parents had a hold on him and I understand how that goes. It did put a dent in my excitement for him. It reminded me how young we were and that his mother was probably right. We're too young to change our lives and continents in order to be together. School and career come first. Love is way down on the list, but it is easier said than done when you're the one in love.

We continued to write until I received a letter from Lorenzo saying his family bought his friend's store. He suggested I don't write there and that I should write to his friend's house instead.

We wrote a few letters and then stopped. I felt like I had nothing to say and the dream of ever being together again was dead. College was all-consuming and working took up any letter writing time. It was too hard to write to someone living this amazing life in an alternate universe while I was struggling, being a mere mortal, paying for college.

It was too depressing. Each letter got more and more difficult to write. Each letter became a reminder of how our lifestyles were so completely different.

There was no hope of us ever being together, and I felt forced to let go of the dream. He was never going to come here if his mother could help it. I was never going to be able to afford to move there or even go there again. Between work and school, it was a hopeless situation. Letting go was almost impossible, but I had to let him go for my sanity.

Could this be true love anyway, at such a young age?

My mother felt terrible that I couldn't go back to keep up the relationship, but she secretly was glad I wouldn't move to Italy permanently. I can't blame either mother, but at least my mother wasn't stealing letters. My mother was livid when she found out about his mother stealing my letters. She felt like his mother thought I wasn't good enough for him and that poorly reflected on her. She was right.

His mother never liked me because I wasn't an Italian socialite or a socialite of any other country. Any time I would mention his mother, my mother would grumble, *"Eh, fa nab, disgraziata"* [go back to Naples, you disgrace]. Back in the day, telling someone to go back to Naples was considered semi-cursing them out. The same as saying, "Go to hell." My mother was right. *Fa nab* to you, lady!

Once we stopped writing, I figured he met someone, got married and had children. I assumed he was living the typical southern

Italian life, which hasn't changed much for centuries.

Unless something drastic happened, I knew he would be fine and have a beautiful life. Throughout the years, I would always try to find Lorenzo on the Internet, but never could. Then one day, years later, it all changed.

Part 6

Return To Italy

Perfect Symphony

When music fails to agree to the ear, to soothe the ear and the heart and the senses, then it has missed its point." Maria Callas

I'm so excited to get back to Italy. This flight feels like it's taking forever. The last years went by fast, but this 9 hour flight to Italy feels like an eternity. While reminiscing about my two summers in Italy, I listened to my whole music library on my IPOD. The last song to play was "Perfect Symphony," by Ed Sheeran and Andrea Bocelli. How fitting for the trip. Some lyrics fit Lorenzo and me perfectly.

I felt like I have lived this song and I'm so glad the plane was a little dark to hide my tears. The lyrics that hit me hardest were the ones that talked about meeting someone as a young person, losing them and then meeting them again when you're older and now trying to fall in love and grieving over the wasted years,

Since it was a long flight, I binge watched Kylie Flavell's YouTube channel. I'm obsessed with her and I was literally living vicariously through *The Dolce Vita Diaries,* videos filmed on the Amalfi Coast. The opening credits alone always put a smile on my face and transport me to another time and place.

While watching her videos, I would pretend I was with her, eating pizza and jumping off the rocks into the crystal blue Mediterranean. In episode 8, she hikes the Path of the Gods. I hoped to be able to hike that again.

I pretended I was with Kylie and looking out over the blue water and feeling like I was transported in time back to the goat herder's camp where we had lunch, wine and perfectly cured meats with Nino and Lorenzo. The views were spectacular. I completely understand how a fresh pea could leave a girl speechless.

I especially loved episode 5, about one of my favorite restaurants in Positano. The restaurant on the beach that cooked cheese on lemon leaves is probably one of the most exquisite plates of food I've ever consumed. How has this been kept a secret from the rest of the world? Her expressions were priceless, and I knew exactly how she felt eating that cheese.

Pure heaven.

The whole Amalfi coast is lemon heaven, not just that one store. To hear Caruso from Lucio Dalla throughout the video made it bittersweet. I was so lost in my imagination; I think I might have belted out a verse while everyone was sleeping on the plane. I would love to meet Kylie and squeeze her cheeks so hard to thank her for the hours of pleasure I have derived while being transported back in time, if even for a few moments.

Torna a Surriento - Return to Sorrento

"Tony Bennett was a consummate artist, all you have to do is listen to any one of his hundreds of recordings to recognize that. Very early on, his music quietly wove itself into the fabric of our lives. His voice felt as familiar and as close as the voices of our loved ones. I know that this was true for millions of people around the world. For Italian Americans who were growing up in the middle of the 20th century, that familiarity ran even deeper. At a certain point, we started to imagine that Tony would live forever. Of course, he didn't. Nobody does. But the music? That's another story." Martin Scorsese

Benvenuti a Italia! Let the butterflies begin. Ahh, Naples airport. The best airport for those of us who hate to fly is beloved Napoli. You practically jump off the plane, walk towards a booth that may or may not have a super hot, confident, manly man waiting to wave you in and welcome you to the most beautiful country in the world. They're so nonchalant about incoming passengers. It's like they would feel intense guilt and shame, even questioning one's desire to take part in God's gift to the world. Welcome to the guts of Italia. I feel like Milan is the mind of Italy, Rome is the heart of Italy and Naples is the guts. As an Italian American, it feels like there is definitely a difference between Naples and the rest of Italy. Milan, Rome and Naples have very distinct personalities. I consider the Neapolitan area to be the ID in a very Freudian way. It's the raw and real part of Italy. It's more primal, aggressive and impulsive, with a little darkness that always seeks pleasure.

We need the ID; we love our ID, but we always need to keep our ID under control. It's wild! If you have Neapolitan friends, you know exactly what I'm talking about. Neapolitans and those of the Campania region are all guts and shoot from the hip. Napoli is the belly of the beast. Most Italian Americans are from the Naples area and Sicily. Sicily is a whole other story. Ha!

Rome is our ego, which is full of logic and constantly trying to keep the ID under control. The ego deals with reality. Milan is the super-ego, which is high class, elegant, intellectual, and very global. Milan is about perfection and being the best.

This goes back to its banking, fashion and religious roots, as it was also one of the most important cities for international business. There is a palpable difference in all 3 areas. They're all beautiful and I prefer the Campania region where Naples is located.

It's literally in my blood. I love the more raw and real energy of the south. Good salt of the earth people. It's the area my family is originally from and so their way of life feels like home to me. I go there and feel like I'm with my people.

Welcome home. *Ciao mi famiglia* [hello my family].

From the airport, I made my way through the crowds trying to get a cab. I was next in line and saw this big smiling face look over at me and waving. He came over and grabbed my suitcase to put in the trunk. He was so chivalrous and he couldn't move fast enough to open the door for me.

I love Italian men! As we drove away, I was so relaxed that I had a nice guy driving me down to Sorrento. What a great way to start my trip!

He started asking about where I was going and what I was doing. His name was Salvatore; he was so happy and full of life. Just like the taxi drivers in New York. Not! I explained to Salvatore I was coming back to Italy to go to San Giovanni Rotondo to see the Padre Pio shrine. His eyes got big and thank God we were sitting in traffic at this point or else he would have stopped short.

He got very excited and told me how much he loves Padre Pio. Then he pulled down his visor and sure enough; he taped a picture of Padre Pio to the back of his visor. We looked at each other in amazement and we both pulled our arms out to show we each got goosebumps at the same time.

We both made the sign of the cross and laughed. Wow, I took it as a sign that I was definitely going to find my way across the country to the shrine to pay respects and hopefully get my miracle, like thousands of other believers, over the last 100 years.

Driving through Naples was pretty cool because it looks like what the meat-packing district of Manhattan looked like in the 80s. It has that rough city vibe, but is full of energy and excitement.

As we were bouncing on the cobblestone streets, Bon Jovi came on the radio and Salvatore blasted "It's My Life" by Bon Jovi.

How fitting; I was in Italy, hoping to reignite my love with Lorenzo while fist pumping to Bon Jovi, and singing with Salvatore.

It was hard to reach the higher octave for the "live forever" part, so we just screamed louder.

Salvatore is already making my trip amazing and I feel like everything is going to work out fine. Fist pumping in Naples to Bon Jovi with my cab driver automatically ranked as one of my favorite travel memories. You can't fabricate, plan, or curate experiences like this, no matter how much money you have.

It's spiritual, special and the magic of Italy.

Finally, I arrived at my glorious hotel, The Grand Hotel Excelsior Vittoria. I can't explain the beauty upon entering this legendary hotel that is still owned by the Fiorentino family. It's located right in the middle of Tasso Square in Sorrento and it overlooks the Gulf of Sorrento. I specifically requested the Enrico Caruso suite where famed opera singer Enrico Caruso stayed for over a month in 1921.

His piano is still there, and this is where Lucio Dalla wrote the song beloved song, Caruso. This was a great way to research two singers for the price of one, all while overlooking the Gulf of Sorrento. There was no other hotel room for me to stay in, in order to find inspiration for my article on some of the greatest Italian opera singers and songs. I'm incredibly grateful that my guy who knows a guy is a really rich guy!

As I was imagining what Lucio Dalla was feeling while he wrote from the balcony of this incredible suite, there was a knock at my door. I thought, "Oh no, he can't be here yet.

What do I do? I still have airplane hair, I haven't changed and my breath is from yesterday's New Jersey mixed with airplane coffee. Please Lord, let this be the rest of my luggage. Wait, I have all my bags, which magically appeared before I even entered my room." Harder and faster knocks on the door.

Oh, God, well, here I go. I give my cheeks a pinch and my tongue a few scrapes with my teeth to try to at least get rid of the coffee taste, so my first kiss with my real-life Fabio after so many years won't be our last.

I gave one last look to my face and wrinkled clothes, took a big gulp of very expensive Caruso suite air and opened the door.

Relief; it's only my gorgeous room attendant with some chilled Prosecco and strawberries. He also brought me a few chilled, lemon-infused smelling towels to wipe the airplane air off my tired face. This was incredibly refreshing and worth the money!

Nothing beats what money can buy and I'm so grateful for Italian compassion for a single American girl chasing a dream, disguised as a writer doing some research. When I checked in, I must have looked like the typical exhausted and slightly frantic American.

Deep breaths. I shot half a glass of Prosecco, chased it with a strawberry, and rushed to the bathroom to repair my makeup and hair. Lord Jesus, where is my toothbrush? I'm dying with the anticipation of seeing Lorenzo again.

He is the man that every man I've dated since him has unknowingly and unsuccessfully been trying to live up to. All I kept thinking was there's no way he's going to like me now. I'm chunkier and older. I have smile lines and didn't have time to Botox my forehead and my curls are slowly turning to frizz.

I hoped that as the sun started its descent, the light wouldn't shine through my hair, making it look too thin and flat.

Shit, he's gotta be married, so why do I even care what he thinks of me? I can't mess around with a married guy. Can I? Should I? Would I? No! No! No! I can't and won't! Do I even want a guy who will cheat on his wife, anyway? Nope. But man, if we have half the chemistry we did all those years ago, how am I going to say, "No" to those aqua-green eyes? I'm a sucker for his eyes and it's the one thing I remember most about my Lorenzo.

Blazing aqua green with hints of Mediterranean blue. If you've ever been to the Amalfi Coast, you know that incredible blue color that is in all the tile floors.

I call it Italian blue. It's like walking on a marble ocean throughout the hotels.

Why on earth did I ever tell him to come to my hotel room to meet me? Ok, like who doesn't want to see the Caruso suite?

I have to admit; I wanted to show off a bit. At the least, maybe he'll be proud of me for having some sort of success and not being a complete failure. Jeez, I need to relax and enjoy the moment because the sun will soon be setting, which is spectacular, romantic and OMG, he's here!

I said yet another prayer for help and hoped Lorenzo would still think I'm cute.

Then, I immediately prayed for forgiveness, because this was not the kind of prayer God would approve of. As I reached for the door handle, I imagined that scene from *The Bridges of Madison County* when Meryl Streep was in the car with her husband.

She had her hand on the car door handle, ready to open the door and run out to the love of her life, Clint Eastwood; but she didn't. She sat there and let what might have been the best move of her life that would finally fulfill her soul drive on by.

I cried for days, thinking of what might have been had she turned the door knob. Now it's my chance to turn the handle of life.

Ti Voglio Bene - I Love You

Before the door was fully opened, Lorenzo's head popped through and his eyes pierced into mine. I don't know if I've ever felt so vulnerable, so purely happy and calm. Wait, what? Calm? Yes, Enzo squeezed through the door opening, never taking his eyes off mine while moving towards me. I gave into the waves of love enveloping me.

His arms felt so strong around me and I can't believe we still haven't said a single word. Just some giggles and mmmm's in such a way that it was understood that our embrace was good, much needed and long overdue.

We stood in the doorway hugging each other, mostly in silence to make up for the last and lost years.

Have you ever held someone, and you just knew? I knew nothing about him or his life now, but it didn't matter because I knew.

I knew the feeling of his arms around my waist. I knew the sturdiness of his shoulders and how his jet black curls would hit the bottom of his jaw and sometimes fall onto my cheek when he would bend over to kiss me. He was holding on to me so tight that I knew he missed me. It was as if he was trying to squeeze us back in time. Time has been good to him. Time is much more kind to men than women.

Neither of us could fully pull away, so we awkwardly half-separated and sat on the bed, still never breaking eye contact. We had to take it all in.

I wanted to know every line, every eyelash, every curl and how it framed his face. His lashes look like the best mascara money could buy. They're so long, thick and curled. It's not fair.

His eyes are spellbinding, and if I looked away, I'd then have to think of something to say. At the moment, my brain was totally empty and incapable of forming a coherent sentence.

He's still so strikingly beautiful. His hands finally left my waist and traveled up my arms, caressed my neck, then his hands cradled the bottom of my jaw while his thumbs outlined my lips. My eyes were half open and I still couldn't bear to break eye contact. I felt my lips half smile. He looked over my face, my lips, my hair and finally back into my eyes and said,

"You look still the same."

Oh, thank-you Jesus, I still got it, I think to myself. He smiled, knowing full well he's teasing me the way only an Italian man can with their confident, killer instinct. They know exactly what women want and need. He makes me vulnerable and forces me into my femininity, which no other man has ever done and I so desperately need. I heard that voice in my head saying, "Let him lead."

Just when I'm about to melt and give in to his lips that left me wanting more for the last decade, the record in my mind skipped, scratched, stopped, and then I remembered he's probably married.

I promised myself 100 times I wouldn't give in so easily, or at all if he's married. It has only been a few minutes since I opened the door and I can see that it's going to be a long two weeks in Italy. Thankfully, he pulled away and stood up to pour us some Prosecco for a toast. After passing me a glass, he slowly took a bite out of a strawberry.

He enjoyed it for a few of the longest seconds ever, then licked his lips as they curled up at the corners with pleasure. He then rubbed the strawberry along the outline of my lips so the juice would drip into my mouth. He placed the strawberry into my mouth to finish and then sucked the juice off his fingers.

I was absolutely dizzy. He took my hand and led me to the legendary balcony to finish watching the sunset. While walking behind him, I watched his open hand glide along the silk upholstered Louis the XVI chairs in front of the fireplace. He was always very tactile and had to touch everything. I used to tell him he wouldn't survive for long if his hands were ever tied behind his back. I smiled at the memory.

We barely spoke, and I didn't mind at all. You would think after so many years, we would be talking a mile a minute to catch up on every detail of our lives. Where had our paths taken us in this thing called life? That is the beauty of the Italian way; enjoy the moment. There is always time to talk, but the sun setting over the Gulf of Sorrento only lasts a few minutes.

Why on earth would anyone ever miss God's moving artwork on display? The details of my life seemed so irrelevant at that moment. I wasn't curing cancer or developing some life-saving app, so why not enjoy the sunset? Italy always brings me back to enjoying life and living in the moment instead of planning how I'm going to orchestrate all of my future moments while this one passes right by me, unnoticed and unappreciated.

In the last seconds of the sun setting, he asked if I remembered the story of Lucio Dalla and Caruso staying here.

"Of course I do, but I'd love to hear it again just in case I forgot any details."

"Ok" he continued in his deep voice that was so musical. He could read the dictionary and it would captivate me.

Very few surpassed his knowledge of the Amalfi Coast. His life as an architect required him to know and obsess on every nook and cranny of every building.

His explanations of the history of the area rolled off his tongue as if he had lived there for a hundred years. I was fascinated with his knowledge, especially of Sorrento or *Surriento* as pronounced in the Neopolitan dialect of which he was well versed.

My Italian was comprised more of the Tuscan style, which I learned in school combined with the New Jersey, Italian-American, which was, um, to say the least, colorful. He always had a good laugh at my expense when I would ask for some food in my American Italian accent. In New Jersey, we all understood our busted, hand-me-down, southern Italian. *Capeeesh* [understand]?

He continued to tell me that in 1986 Dalla was so inspired by Caruso's favorite room at the Grand Excelsior and the Gulf of Sorrento, he wrote the song Caruso. Dalla even said, "Sorrento is the true corner of my soul." I had to agree.

The song is a masterpiece and it would inspire you as well while sitting on this balcony. Luciano Pavarotti and Julio Iglesias even did a cover of the song. Pavarotti sold over 9 million copies and Andrea Bocelli's first album sold over 20 million copies featuring the song Caruso. Lara Fabian also did a hauntingly beautiful rendition. It's quite spectacular.

Another singer who totally nails this song is Florent Pagny. Over the years, I had become a little obsessed with this song. Every time I heard it, it brought me right back to my first summer on the raft with Lorenzo.

The song Caruso was an homage to the great tenor Enrico *Caruso*. The composition is "*spettacolo*" [spectacular] according to Lorenzo.

I could not disagree. I also prefer the original, sung by Dalla. Pavarotti is in a category all his own and sometimes he is too perfect, but Dalla's voice cracks just enough that you know someone was in great pain and longing without understanding a word. Dalla must have drawn from his own early musical experiences. He was not always well-received by Italians. Some even threw rotten tomatoes at his face while he was performing. This had to have some effect on a performer, and yet he kept going.

Towards the end of his life, you can see the pain in his face, even as the fans are obsessing over his voice. Rejection always stings and stays with the soul. The words of the song are so inspiring because I have also looked out into the Gulf of Sorrento and cried for a lost love. Here I am, yet again coming back for more.

As beautiful as the lyrics are, there is one cello version by Stjepan Hauser that will bring anyone to tears. You can tell Stjepan totally feels the pain and beauty of "Caruso."

This song had a hauntingly familiar feel to it and I couldn't understand why until Lorenzo told me that the chorus is similar to the opera song, "Dicitencello Vuie" written in 1930 by Enzo Fusco. Francesco Albanese made this song very popular when he sang it in the 1940s. Lorenzo explained who Albanese was, and I remembered hearing this song before sung by my father's favorite singer, Mario Lanza.

Alabanese has a much more Neapolitan way of singing with the traditional staccato stanzas that break up the flow of a traditional opera songs flow. I couldn't wait to learn more about Albanese and I felt like my story was unfolding right before my eyes. It was so exciting and it felt like an Italian treasure hunt. It was surprising to learn Francesco sang with the great Maria Callas. His Neapolitan style and her classical, traditional style would seemingly clash, but they didn't. I would love to write about Callas, but she was Greek, not Italian. I would have to save her for the next article.

I love the Italian saying, "*Ti voglio bene*," which is also the chorus for Dalla's song. It basically translates to, "I want good for you." This is how Italians say, "I love you," for a friendship kind of love. I think this is beautiful and sad that we don't say this to our friends.

We only say, "I love you," to the people we are romantically involved with. A true love wants good for you and is unselfish. "I love you" is all about my feelings and me and totally selfish. It's subtle but oh so different. Maybe this is where most love relationships go wrong. At the base, they're selfish and about our own feelings.

We don't always want good for the others more than we want good for ourselves. The song talks about a man watching his love leave out of the Gulf of Sorrento on a boat and he is devastated and suffocating from the pain. Typical Italian drama.

The sun finally lost its battle to the horizon. The remaining light reflected from the moon, the fishing boat lights, and the stars.

Lorenzo turned to face me and leaned back against the balcony railing, so the light from the moon illuminated his head like a halo.

He tilted his head to the side and asked me, "Are you happy?"

I softly responded, "Right now, I am blissful."

This was my way of being in the moment and deflecting the real question. I would not be let off so easily. He leaned in so the halo disappeared and the light bounced off his green eyes into mine so there was nowhere left to hide. He was so intent on my answer; I froze.

I felt like a little girl getting into trouble. Oh boy, he was trouble. At the same time, I couldn't look away, since he was only a few inches from my face.

I couldn't lie and say I was truly happy, but I didn't want to burst into ugly tears and look like an emotional basket case. He doesn't know that I'm known for being an emotional stone. I'm not one for emotional wishy-washy stuff. My face was getting red and hotter by the millisecond.

I wanted to burst out how much I've always loved him and how I'm so sorry we lost touch and how no man has ever been able to live up to him, but all I could do was nod my head slightly up and down to motion yes, and whisper, "and you?"

He answered, "Right now, I am-a bliss-a-ful."

Looks like neither of us wanted to answer that question. We both smiled half smiles and didn't say a word. We silently breathed deeply the beautiful fresh air of Sorrento.

Life happens and when we lost touch years ago, I thought I was going to be some trend setting music journalist, working with celebrities and writing for Rolling Stone, The Village Voice or Billboard Magazine. A permanent seat at The MTV Awards was definitely in my future. I loved Italy, and I loved Lorenzo, but I had big things to accomplish in America. Years of failed relationships, difficult jobs, and missed opportunities took their toll on me. Not for nothing; I was not happy.

To admit that to someone else and to say it out loud would make it all too real. I felt like a sloppy mess under his green-eyed gaze. On the outside, it did look like I was doing well and technically, I was, but not as well as I had hoped. I had big dreams.

People only saw the highlights, not the failures or struggles to get there.

I noticed he wasn't wearing a ring. He was more the rugged outdoor type, so I didn't think anything of it. The tension between us was palpable and I don't remember ever being so nervous, so giddy, and so unable to express myself. Somehow, it felt completely normal to stand in the comfort of silence together.

After what seemed like an eternity, he backed up to the balcony's edge and the halo found its rightful place behind his jet-black curls.

"So what are your plans for the next 2 weeks?" he asked.

Ahh, saved by mundane details. Now, I can actually speak a full sentence.

"Well, I need to gather as much behind-the-scenes information as possible about some of the greatest Italian opera singers. I need the stories behind the best songs to present to an Italian American Association.

I figured coming here to where it all started would be the best place to get inspired and hopefully get some stories you can't find in the books or on Google."

"And that is the only reason?"

Damn, why does he keep cornering me like this? Why is he teasing me if this romance can't go anywhere? Reliving the past is so painful when the present is a total disconnect from where I hoped I'd be by now.

"What more reasons could a girl need than Italy, opera, food, wine and love?"

Yikes! I quickly recovered and said, "the love of Sorrento, Positano."

Whew, I think he bought it at least for a few seconds. He winked and half smirked at me, letting me know he caught onto my verbal gymnastics, even in English.

"I hope we can spend some time together. You can show me around a little when you're free. I mean, I realize you have a family and it's ok if you can't spend…"

Enzo started to shake his head back and forth and raised his hands in a windshield wiper motion.

He moved in closer and once again held my face by my jaw. He put his thumbs over my lips to stop me from speaking and said,

"No, you are-a my guest in *mi citta'* bella [my beautiful city] and I take-a care of you."

All I could do was smile the biggest smile. The kind of smile filled with relief, anticipation and joy. I could feel my cheeks hitting my bottom lashes and my top lashes hit my eyelids while looking up at him with big doll eyes.

He pulled my head down towards him so he could kiss my forehead and then pulled me in and wrapped his arms around my upper back and squeezed me so tightly. We both started laughing so hard, it made ending the hug so much less awkward. Thank God for that.

He then took the obligatory big breath as if saying, this has to end now before walking towards the door to leave. I was relieved, but a little disappointed. My real-life Hallmark movie came to a crashing halt.

I kept reminding myself that he's married and I don't want a married man. I never felt like he was the cheating type. If he did make moves on me, I'd be so happy for the first kiss, and then disappointed that he's like every other guy. I couldn't bear the thought my Lorenzo was like every other loser.

As he reached for the door handle, he turned his head back toward me and said,

"What time should I pick you up tomorrow?"

"Uh, I don't know. Where are we going and what are we doing?"

"We are writing your article."

"Really? WE are?" I chuckled.

"Yes, let me lead the way and you will see."

That was music to my tired, love worn ears. That's what I loved about him from years ago; I didn't have to make all the decisions.

I didn't always have to be in control and I didn't have to lead. He allowed me to be a woman by his very nature of being the man; literally.

"Ok, you lead and I will follow you, Lorenzo," I said, with a little wink and shoulder raise. My grandmother Virginia would often "give the shoulder" as we would call it.

Every time I do it, I giggle a bit, thinking she would be proud of me for giving someone the shoulder. It's a little raising of the shoulder that could be cold and dismissive, sexy and sultry or cute and flirty.

I was definitely going for cute and flirty, but a little sexy might have snuck out.

"Allora, 9am to eat, then-a we go."

"Ok, buona notte."

And that was that. My first encounter with Lorenzo after many years was over.

Too tired to take a shower and too awake to sleep, I grabbed the rest of the strawberries and Prosecco, and plopped onto the bed to replay every single luscious, minute detail of the evening.

Memory Lane

"I wish some of my memories were scratch and sniff." - Lora Condon

Did you ever wake up with a smile on your face? It's the most amazing feeling when you're completely peaceful and serene in those few moments before you're fully conscious. The chilly morning breeze was off-set by the sun directly hitting my feet, giving me the perfect balance of warm and cool. It made me feel like Italy was kissing my feet while lovingly brushing my hair from my eyes; welcoming me back like a beloved old friend.

I looked over towards the open balcony door and realized I had overslept. Lorenzo is going to be here in a half hour and I haven't even showered. I started rushing around like a maniac, trying to find the perfect outfit for whatever he might have planned for today. Bless this breeze right now or else I'd be sweating to death before I even made it downstairs.

In true female fashion, I was 10 minutes late getting to the lobby and electric with anticipation for the day ahead. While walking down the marble staircase, a breeze strong enough to raise my skirt up my thigh swept across the lobby. I was able to save myself from epic embarrassment by catching my skirt before it blew all the way up. I might not have been as swift as I thought due to all the men in the lobby grinning and staring to see if there was going to be an instant replay or, hopefully, another, stronger breeze.

Lorenzo was waiting for me at the bottom of the stairs, grinning along with the rest of the men. He put his arm out like a true gentleman to save me from further embarrassment; like face planting on the last marble step.

We walked out of the hotel right into the heart of Sorrento for a cappuccino and pastry. I couldn't think of a better way to start the day. Our conversations were somewhat basic and composed of me asking him questions about opera singers, living in Italy and any other generic topic I could think of to postpone talking about where we left off years ago, how we lost touch and of course, his wife.

Walking around the heart of Sorrento for a few hours is one of my favorite things to do, and here I was doing it with one of my favorite people. It was as if time stood still. The town is so alive with the smell of fresh lemons, charred pizza crust and bakeries all mixed with the softest leather. I can't believe no one has bottled this scent and created a perfume called Sorrento. While Lorenzo took a phone call, I found a gorgeous fragrance in a perfume store. The store was small but jam-packed with all different fragrances created by the owner. I picked up a few and the last one I picked up was labeled Caruso. I'm pretty sure this has to be my scent. As I sprayed it, the owner came over and told me this was her creation to honor Enrico Caruso. She asked me if I was familiar with the singer. I replied I was very familiar, and that I was even staying in his suite at the Grand Excelsior.

Her face lit up as she said, "Wow, this must be a very special trip for you. That is no ordinary room."

I explained the article I was writing, which included Enrico Caruso's music and life. I told her about my two summers in Punta Massa years ago and how I was visiting my friend Lorenzo. She knew exactly who Lorenzo was.

She froze, looked at me and asked, "You're the Americana he fell in love with all those years ago?"

"Yes, that's me, I think; L'americana," I responded. She hugged me and told me how happy she was that I was back. The rumor was he never got over me, and his mother was taking my letters. She mentioned it was so mean to do to her son.

She immediately pulled an unopened Caruso off the shelf, wrapped it up and insisted I take it as a welcome back gift. I graciously took the gift. Suddenly Enzo walked in and she had to ask him how I ended up coming back to Sorrento.

He gave her the brief explanation, which kind of meant that he didn't want to explain anymore. She caught on and let us leave the store without explaining the end of my last trip or what was in store for the rest of this trip.

When we left, Lorenzo groaned, "She's always-a so busy, busy busy, in everyone else-a business."

"Well, she seems happy for you and even gave me this perfume as a welcome back gift. I can't complain about her," I said, smiling and flinging my perfume bag around in the air. He smirked back at me, but he obviously felt the less they all knew, the better.

Next, we went to Sapori e Calori for the best homemade limoncello. I love this store because you get to try some limoncello while you shop! There's always time for limoncello and it's never too early to be drinking when you're on vacation. Their beautiful hand-painted ceramic bottles make amazing gifts.

I got a few bottles for my mom and for the guy who know the guys who got me here. I especially loved the bottles shaped like Italy and always made sure to get a few of those bottles for extra gifts. On this visit, I also found the most incredible chocolate balls filled with limoncello. I don't know where these little balls of love were hiding all my life, but these definitely are coming back to America with me.

Each store brought back a memory. As we passed each restaurant, I could automatically remember exactly what I had eaten there.

There aren't enough meals in a month to eat in all the restaurants I want to eat. We passed the beautiful Ristorante o Parrucchiano La Favorita, which is now called I Giardini di Tasso, where I first learned that Italians eat dinner at 9pm. Americans consider this absurd, but with the hours I work, ironically, that tends to be the time I'm finally able to eat my dinner. We decided to go in and get some lunch. The restaurant looks like any other restaurant from the outside, but when you walk in; it becomes a beautiful lemon grove with tables under the lemon trees and little lights strewn through the trees for the most romantic experience.

Lorenzo told me it was originally a Roman aqueduct and the atmosphere definitely makes you feel like you're eating in a ancient cave of lemon-filled history. The ravioli with lemon sauce and fried zucchini flowers made the perfect lunch, along with some red wine. In a country where wine can be cheaper than water, what could be better than indulging all day long.

Once again, I tried to bring the conversation back to opera while he kept diverting to food, wine and southern Italian living. I asked him about Beniamino Gigli, who sang one of my favorite songs, "Una Furtiva Lagrima." Lorenzo mentioned that Gigli was very fond of Padre Pio and Padre Pio would make him sing the song "Mamma" for him when he visited San Giovanni Rotondo in honor of his mother.

Yes!!!! I finally found a Padre Pio connection for the article. I also found out that Andrea Bocelli was going to sing at the Padre Pio shrine in San Giovanni Rotondo in a few days to celebrate Padre Pio.

I hit the Catholic Italian opera jackpot!

Beniamino rose to fame after Enrico Caruso died in 1921. They are often compared, but don't sound the same to me at all. Gigli's voice is not full and robust like Pavarotti or powerful, clear and strong like Caruso's or Lanza's voice. It has a fragile vibrato that also makes it very distinctive. His unique voice is also what makes his version of "Una Furtiva Lagrima" the best, in my opinion. It gives the song a sad, longing feeling that leaves one wanting more. Not every singer and every song needs to be full blast the whole time in order to be great.

I would have loved to hear him sing Dalla's song "Caruso" for this very reason.

Gigli often performed at the New York Metropolitan Opera House. When he refused to take a pay cut, he returned to Italy to perform and had so many fund-raising concerts in which he raised more money than any other singer in history at the time, with close to one thousand benefit concerts.

They gave much of the money raised to Padre Pio's charitable causes. Deeply spiritual, Gigli visited Padre Pio in San Giovanni Rotondo many times, which is way out of the way and difficult to get to, especially back then. Gigli also sang many sacred songs which was not typical of opera singers in the 1950s.

Gigli's love life… well, that was not so sacred. In typical male fashion, he had a few wives and lots of kids. Serious baby mamma drama!

On a whim, I asked Lorenzo to go to the Padre Pio shrine for a few days in San Giovanni Rotondo. Like an answered prayer, he automatically responded, "Yes." His eyes lit up as he stood a little straighter. We immediately started creating a plan to go across the country for a few days on a pilgrimage to see Padre Pio's church right before I left. Suddenly, Lorenzo had an odd look on his face that I had never seen before. I couldn't put my finger on what he was feeling or thinking and I thought maybe it was me being overly sensitive. This was amazing, and it felt like God was bringing us there.

I couldn't wait to call my parents and hear their reactions. My heart was so full. I was floating. I'm here in Sorrento, Italy with the man of my dreams that I've waited 10 years to be with and now we're going to one of the most important sites in all of modern Christlandom. Over six million people a year go to visit the shrine and to learn about the miracles that have taken place in San Giovanni Rotondo, through Padre Pio.

My cheeks hurt from smiling and my face was actually hot to the touch from the adrenaline rush. Never in my life has everything ever come together like this.

The magic of Italy never disappoints and today is no different.

There is nothing like walking around Sorrento in a state of bliss. We walked and hiked around all day. After making our way to the top of a few cliffs to catch the best views of the area, we decided it was time to go down to the Marina Grande to Soul and Fish Restaurant for some seafood and more wine.

As we made our way down to the marina, we talked with the fishermen about what they were catching and drooled over the day's catch. This restaurant is always a winner. Their location gives you the opportunity to look out at the water, as well as people watch. We like all the same food, so we got a few different dishes and shared everything. I let him order his white Campania wine, and I got my red Campania wine. We started with perfectly grilled *polpo* [octopus] and grilled vegetables. That is such a difficult dish to make because most overcook the polpo and then it gets rubbery and the veggies become *mushad* [mushy]. Then we shared an incredible moist and thick sea bass prepared at the table with crab linguini *al dente*. You need to have some macaroni at least once a day.

After dinner, we opted for espresso and resting at the end of the dock. Once again, it feels like I blinked and went from sitting in dirty Jersey to sitting on the dock in Sorrento looking at Vesusvio on my right and Capri on my left. The history between us and Sorrento did not go unnoticed. It was incredibly deep and full of tragedy, but able to rise from the ashes after all.

I felt like we were in a little bubble at the end of that dock. The restaurants were full, and the dock was buzzing with fisherman and hungry tourists. All I could see and hear was Lorenzo. Sitting so close, I hoped he couldn't feel my heart pounding. All I wanted to do was to kiss and hug him.

Once again, we didn't talk much, and I had nothing else to say except, "I love you, still," which, of course, I never dared to vocalize. This was the perfect atmosphere because the setting sun in Italy is spectacular. Whatever the sun hits turns gold. I can only imagine what the ancient Romans thought when the sky would turn hot pink and the cliffs and ruins would turn rose gold. *Spettacolo* [spectacular]. As we were settling into waiting for the sun to set, he grabbed my hand, pulled me up and started walking towards the car.

"Where are we going? That was so nice there," I said.

He stopped walking, looked me dead in the eye and said, "Yes, but I know some place better, trust me."

How could I not?

While driving, I noticed we were on a cliff getting closer to the edge. It felt like we were going alongside the edge of the mountain when suddenly, a very familiar feeling started to come over me. The sun was still dancing on the ocean, illuminating it in the most beautiful way. He started to slow down due to the steeper turns and around the last curve, there it was.

My heart stopped. I gasped at the site of the most incredible three black jetties right off the shore protecting the homes of

Punta Massa. This is the sleepy beach town of the Sorrento Penninsula, where I spent 2 summers romancing away with Lorenzo, in the Gulf of Naples.

I couldn't believe he was bringing me back to the villa. The sun was just about to set.

I have major butterflies in my stomach right now. What could be more romantic than going back to where we started? One of the few pictures I have of us is the first time we went out on the yacht to swim near Capri. All the memories came rushing back; the thought of what could have been, made me start crying. He grabbed my hand, and we looked at each other.

He knew exactly what I was feeling. This was so special and there is no one else in the world I would rather be with right now than Lorenzo. I would never come back here alone, ever.

I choked on the tears of regret and the pain of wasted years trying to be the typical, successful American. Now I'm coming to the realization that this so-called success did not make me feel fulfilled.

Ma La Notte, No or Maybe, Yes

"My kiss will dissolve the silence that makes you mine." Nessun Dorma

I couldn't wait to get out of the car and kiss the ground. My sweet Punta Massa. Everyone writes about Sorrento or Positano, but this is where I left my heart. The town of the three black jetties holds my second true heart. I wondered if my hair clip Enzo dropped years ago was still stuck in the rocks. Such a silly thought as the tears kept falling down my cheek dropping onto my chest.

He knows me well enough to know that I'm uncomfortable with such personal displays of emotion and looking so vulnerable. He also knows me well enough to know that I can't hide myself from him.

I can only contain years of pent-up love for so long and it was here looking down at the jetties from the top of the mountain that made me mourn my American life. We drove all the way to the end of town, right to the edge of the protected reserve to the very house I spent my two summers on the Amalfi Coast.

Again, he grabbed my hand and led me down the stairs to the water's edge so I could see the house I used to stay in for those two amazing summers. Walking along the concrete barrier between the summer homes and the ocean was, "Like déjà vu all over again," as Yogi Berra would say. It was surreal, comforting, wild and scary.

I had so many conflicting emotions and my eyes must have been huge taking it all in. Every step had some special memory. I turned my head to the left where the homes were all lined up with the ocean on my right. We unconsciously slowed down our walk until I spotted the ceramic square of tile art on the home that I loved so much.

In the midst of the old and now slightly crumbling wall was the tile identifying the home. There it was, the beautiful hand-painted dragonfly tile embedded into the wall next to the doorframe.

I stopped and breathed in so deeply trying to inhale and get back what I left there so long ago. I put my hand over the tile, touching it like I used to, hoping it would magically bring me back in time.

Then I put my forehead against the tile and the coolness felt so refreshing and I wished I could start all over from the beginning. I couldn't.

Yet somehow, here I was with Lorenzo once again. Could this be a new start? He put his hand over mine. As he moved closer behind me, he held my other hand that was unconsciously clenched into a fist that I didn't even notice until he tried to hold it.

"You know I feel the same-a, yes? I miss you my libellula so much and I could never bring myself to come back here to visit after you left for the last time."

Still holding my hands, he slowly turned me around like a ballerina in an old Italian music box playing, "Torna a Surriento."

As I looked up at him, I could feel my eyes getting wet and about to cry. I closed my eyes and inhaled so deeply that when I exhaled; it felt like my shoulders dropped an inch. Before I opened my eyes, I felt Lorenzo lean closer into me. He now positioned both of my hands above my head against the wall, and I could feel the cold dragonfly tile against my arm. I never wanted this moment to end. Do I open my eyes or not?

I could feel his body pressing against mine, letting osmosis do its thing that it does so well. I couldn't open my eyes. I was afraid it was all a dream. Oh, please God, don't let this end. I feel like Vesuvious right now.

This girl has been rumbling for years and is ready to explode. His cheek touched mine and I could feel him moving to whisper in my ear. Finally, the words I've been longing to hear him say.

"Mariella, I have been-a waiting my whole-a life for you to come back to me, my libellula."

He said this in such a musical, sarcastic way, I expected him to say, "You naughty girl, why you-a tease a-me like this?"

He continued more seriously, saying, "Now, I have-a you and I want to-a finish what we had-a so long ago. Ella, please do not-a make me wait any longer."

With my eyes still closed, he put both of my hands into the palm of his one hand and then he put his free hand under my chin and gently tilted my face up towards him. I opened my eyes just in time to see him leaning in to kiss me. Eyes wide open because neither of us wanted to miss this magical moment. We've waited too long.

My stomach was doing flips, and my heart was pounding. I think I might have dug my fingers into his back, but neither of us cared.

It was like the floodgates burst open and our passion flowed like lava over each other as we played out our own dramatic opera. We made up for all those years in one long kiss and embrace that would have crushed most people's ribs. His breathing got heavier and his hands gripped me so tightly.

Every time he pulled me closer, I would moan as he pushed the breath out of my lungs. His voice was so deep with pleasure while moving around, trying to kiss every inch of my face and neck.

He threw his jacket on the ground and picked me up. I wrapped my legs around his waist and held onto his broad, steady shoulders.

I remember this position quite well and I knew exactly how to position my hands on his muscles so we would not topple over. We balanced against the wall without missing a beat. Before I could come up for air, he held me tighter and brought me down onto his jacket; my legs still wrapped around him. Yes, this is a Hallmark movie and then some. I wish I could say I was a good girl and resisted, but there was no way I was letting my last chance to relive my youth with the love of my life slide right on by. God forgive me, but a girl can only resist so much.

He cleverly slid my dress up a little as his whole body came down on top of me. I felt all the air leave my lungs right into his mouth and it created suction between us forcing our lips and mouths to stick together. We both started giggling like school kids and it gave me a chance to actually catch my breath.

"Mmmmmari-ella, you are more beautiful now more than ever and I want you now more than ever."

His teeth took a hold of the zipper on my dress and he slowly moved it down as he inhaled me and stopped to kiss me inch by inch. As my top opened and he visually took in what I had to offer, a perfect breeze came along and danced on my body, creating a heavenly sensation against his warm lips and tongue.

As an architect, it was like he was using his tongue to savor every curve and the composition of my body in a way that no other man has done before.

He slowly moved his tongue around in a way that let me know

he was memorizing every inch of the landscape so he could draw pictures in his mind for future use.

A girl knows when a man really loves her and when he is out for only himself. It's the magic key that opens a woman's heart, mind and body. As he opened me up, there was no need for resistance, doubt, or questions. It was as if nothing changed. We had our perfect chemistry and moved like ballroom dancers that have been dancing together for years. Anticipating each other's next move to create the most beautiful and fluid shapes. I forgot how long he could last and I wasn't about to rush anything this side of heaven. Every thrust had meaning and intention behind it.

Every moan was a direct result of pure mutual pleasure. I know I've never been so happy; at least since the last time I was with Lorenzo. We fit together perfectly. No man ever made me feel so loved, wanted, and desired. Being apart made no sense anymore and there was nothing left I had to learn by being alone without my love.

It was only then, after all this time, that I believed he felt for me everything that I had been feeling for him. He really loved me. It wasn't only a fun summer fling. I think because we were so young, we figured it was only fun and then we would find our "real loves" and live happily ever after, or at least the lives everyone expected us to live. I know his family had no expectations of him marrying an American girl and my family had no intentions of letting me move to another country, even if it was It-ly.

Looking back and having loved and lost, I think we both realized in that moment that we were each other's "real love" and what we had was real. As we kissed and held each other, all I could keep saying was, "*Mi dispiace*, Enzo, *Mi dispiace*, that I never came back. I don't know why I was so stupid. I was so young and had no idea what love really was. I never thought it would be you. *Mi dispiace, mi dispiace.*"

My breathing was so labored and staccato; like a toddler having a fit and sucking up enough air to make my whole body shudder up and down, even under the weight of his beautiful body.

"My beautiful libellula, Ella," he calmed me by holding my entire face with one of his hands. "It's ok, my Ella, it's ok. We were a so young and-a who would have-a thought? True love and our love is-a like the Amalfi Coast. This is-a God's gift to us."

His wise calmness, sound demeanor was so refreshing and so opposite of me. I need him. He's so good for me, I thought to myself. Finally, I caught my breath, and I felt like I was still a young girl and he had grown up into a mature, stable man. Imagine that! He is still everything I want and need.

The moonlight and fisherman's lights caught his hair and created a halo. Now, I know he's an angel. We were in total peace in each other's arms, lying on his jacket on top of the concrete ocean barrier.

It felt like I was lying on the puffiest of clouds that heaven could offer.

Once the euphoria subsided, I got the courage to speak and address the next hurdle. I couldn't think of some creative or passive, gentle way to ask about his wife, so I blurted out, "What about your wife?"

Boom. A deadly silence filled the air.

"Mariella," he exclaimed.

He sounded like my grandmother when she couldn't believe I said something vulgar or crass.

"Do you think I would be here making-a love to you like this if I was still married? Do you not-a know me at all?"

Well, now, I felt like a total idiot who betrayed him. I'm the one who knowingly slept with a married person, not knowing he wasn't married anymore.

"Sorry, I thought you were still married, and that is why you never tried to reach out to me. I don't know what to think; I have no idea."

"The day you emailed-a me was the same-a day I left my fiance for good. I never married. We are more friends, not lovers. We were too young-a and grew apart. Maybe, eh we were never right for each other. She's cold-a and calculating, and we have-a no passion.

I have-a dream for my future. I want to open my own-a architecture firm and travel. She wants to be a socialite, rule the Amalfi Coast, and-a gossip at parties. I was dying a very slow death. Our parents pressured us to be together when we were very young, since we grew up in the same town and our families have known each other forever.

I thought maybe I would fall in love with her, but it never happened. My creative spirit was-a killed and-a no passion. I need to fulfill my passions. An Italian man with-a no passion is not a man at all. Seeing you and kissing you again is bringing me back-a to life. I remember every moment. Since you emailed me all I can think about is our summers together, my old dreams and how I was going to be a famous architect.

Restoring crumbling buildings and being known all-a over Europe for keeping Italy's history a-beautiful, restored and relevant is-a my passion. I have success with work, but not enough and no love."

To me, he just got infinitely more beautiful. Immediately, my mind started racing with possibilities. Surprisingly, we somehow ended up here, helping each other to rekindle the passion and fire that was in our veins. I had to ask the ill-fated question, "So, where does that leave us?"

"Together," he replied, "and do not worry how. You know you

can leave-a that to me and God will make it happen. *Italia* is magical, don't you feel it?"

"Oh, Enzo, I feel your magic for sure."

His eyes sparkled as he winked at me and wiggled a little since he was still inside me. That was all the spark he needed to go again.

After a few hours, I was exhausted, dehydrated and exhilarated. "I look a mess", I said.

He replied softly singing back imitating Andrea Bocelli, "My darling, you look perfect tonight."

Art imitating life or the other way around? It was perfect. The cool ocean air wrapping around my body gave me relief from the heat of his body on mine. It was the most lovely combination ever.

I could have stayed wrapped up all night long. Eventually, we got up and headed back to the gorgeous Caruso suite, closing the door on the last 10 years and opening up the door to the next.

Music Box History

"When I open the music box and close my eyes, I'm immediately back in Sorrento." Lora Condon

The next morning, we headed out to do more research on great opera singers from the Neapolitan area. I actually did have to do some work to justify my trip. While walking around the shops of Sorrento, we went into a tiny store called Gargioulo Inlaid, by Salvatore. This store had all handcrafted, inlaid wood music boxes, watches and hanging wall art. The care and love that went into each piece is beyond anything a machine can do.

I decided on a wall hanging of the famous Pieta sculpture by Michelangelo and a wooden watch for my father. I had to open almost every music box and listen to the songs. My favorites were always "Torna a Surriento" and "Volare".

I was having a blast reliving my youth because every Italian American has some of these incredible pieces of artwork in their house growing up. Now, here I am again with an even greater appreciation of the craft.

These songs warm my heart to no end. Hearing Enzo hum and sing the songs reminded me of how we would sing songs together while in the town square and the gentle moments with him singing Italian love songs to me. He was always singing and full of happiness and passion.

This store reminded me of one years ago in Sorrento called Gabriella. I bought the most beautiful inlaid wood wall hanging with an image of Jesus. When my mother was there years ago, she bought the most beautiful inlaid wood side tables. She also bought a huge card table with two chairs and had them shipped back to America.

It also had a roulette wheel deep down in the table that was revealed after taking the top off and two layers of inlaid wood. Each layer had a game on it or felt for cards, checkers or chess.

It's an authentic piece of art that is priceless by today's standards. She bought this in the late 1970s, so I grew up loving this style of Italian handcrafted art. We all had our very own inlaid wood musical jewelry box with a little ballerina inside that would spin when the music played. My piece had "Torna a Surriento" and my sister's had "Arrivaderci Roma." I think every opera singer has sung these songs.

They're instant classics. My mother would bring back music boxes or music tables as gifts to people every time she went to Italy. They never understood the value or appreciated the gift until they went to Italy themselves and then the music became your very own escape into paradise every time you lifted the lid. Looking back, it's kind of prophetic that my song was, "Torna A Surriento."

It made me wonder about the history of the songs and how they could fit into my article. After doing a little research, I found out that "Torna a Surriento" or "Come Back to Sorrento." was composed in 1902 by Italian musician, Ernesto De Curtis. His brother Giambattista De Curtis, who was a poet and painter, wrote the lyrics.

They're the original Elton John and Bernie Taupin. Supposedly, Guglielmo, mayor of Sorrento asked Giambattista to write a song for the Prime Minister Giuseppe Zanardelli, to honor him while he was on vacation and staying at the Imperial Hotel Tramontano in Sorrento. Some say the song proclaims the beauty of Sorrento as a plea to get a desperately needed updated sewage system. People also say they wrote the song approximately 8 years before they claimed to have written it based on a copy sent to the Italian Society of Authors and Editors. In true Italian fashion, nothing is ever as it seems. There is always drama.

Lorenzo and his family met many of the famous guests staying at these hotels while they strolled the streets of Sorrento for inspiration, love, and killer shopping. The artists, writers and royalty loved the shops of Sorrento because they're all unique artisans bringing the best of Italy all to one city.

The ability to create your signature scent in Lorenzo's store was a hit with the wealthy. One-of-a-kind, couture cologne is priceless, and some recipes were so unique and desired that the royal or wealthy would not allow that recipe to ever be replicated or sold to anyone but them. Of course, this came at a price, but exclusivity is worth it for those with an ego as big as their bank account. It was no ordinary fragrance store. Working in the store and being around this atmosphere, catering to all kinds of people his whole life, gave Lorenzo his unique ability to be so confident. He immediately knew how to speak to each person on their social level and what words and body language to use to make them feel comfortable. It was as if they spoke the same language, no matter what language they spoke.

To the wealthy women, he would stress the exclusivity of customization and how their other wealthy and famous friends would be so jealous to know a company in Italy is making a perfume, especially for them.

For the average woman, he would tell them how a certain scent brought out their inner beauty and made them unforgettable. For the wealthy men, their specific cologne was a chick magnet and for the average men, the specific cologne was a chick magnet!

Men are simple like that. It also gave him the ability to see how money is only energy and does not define who you are, as many people believe. He could instantly read people and know what they want. This is an incredible blessing for business and love. In someone with low morals, this talent could make someone sociopathic or a used car salesman type. Enzo was neither.

He was grounded and well-balanced. He was more of a people pleaser without losing himself, like many do. Yet he was no push-over, that's for sure. His dealings with the wealthiest people of the world made him want to play down his wealth and connections. He saw the trappings and saw how unhappy most of them were, despite having the best of everything at their fingertips.

He always said, "Money makes you more of what you already are. If you're a good person, you'll be better. If you're a bad person, you'll be worse. It only makes your personality more intense, for good or bad." I had to agree.

While going over the songs in my head, I totally related to the lyrics of "Torna a Surriento." I don't know if there is another place on earth where the actual land of the country itself is difficult to leave. There is a magnetic pull to Sorrento, and it wants to love you.

It's a jealous lover and punishes you for leaving by piercing a gaping hole in your heart and soul. You're never complete until you return. I always felt like I was the only person who felt like I was cheating on Sorrento. When you listen to the words of these old songs, you realize that there are many of us who have cheated on Sorrento and paid dearly by spending the rest of our lives begging for forgiveness and promising to never leave it again.

The lyrics of "Torna A Surriento" express the longing so well which is why everyone sighs a big loud sigh when this song plays in a restaurant or theater in America.

I understood the pain very well, but I couldn't find a way to get back and to make a clean break to move there. Italy is always running through my mind and through my heart. It would be my pleasure to spend the rest of my life here begging Sorrento for forgiveness.

As we made our way around Sorrento, I passed a sign pointing to Figaro's Barber Shop. Now, that's funny, I thought to myself. Who doesn't love singing "Figaro, Figaro, Figaro?" It always reminds me of when Bugs Bunny would sing it. The sign wouldn't make any sense unless you realized the name of the opera is, *Figaro, The Barber of Seville*.

I wonder how many thousands of people walked by that sign and had no clue. Although Mozart wrote the opera, the aria, "Largo al Factotum." was written by an Italian, Gioachino Rossini. Rossini composed 34 operas and didn't even work for the last 40 years of his life. Astounding creativity in such a short amount of time.

He was also a political activist and imprisoned two separate times due to his activism. On the other end of the scope, he helped to create and promote comedic opera or opera *buffa,* as it's called in Italian, which is the genre of "Figaro." A complex man, for sure.

Walking around Sorrento only does one thing to a girl, and that is to make her hungry. It's time for my favorite part of the day. I also couldn't believe we hadn't been to Lorenzo's store yet. I asked him if he wanted to go or if he was hiding me, to which his face looked confused. "Mariella, my family is waiting for us to go to lunch."

Can this man have any more surprises? I was completely speechless. A big smile came across my face and wouldn't leave.

"Wow, I'm so excited. Wait, even your mother?" I had to ask.

"I mean, she did take my letters and hide them from you, so we would break up. It worked because you ended up marrying someone and that person was not me."

"Yes, they are all-a waiting in the store and-a then we go to-a lunch. My mother knows she was-a wrong."

"Yeah, now, years later!"

"*Meglio tardi che mai, no?*" [better late than never,no?] "*Non, ti preoccupare.*" [don't you worry].

He pinched my cheek, kissed my forehead, and led me down the street to the perfume store where we first met. Every step was like slow motion. I could feel the corner of each cobblestone hitting the bottom of my foot through the sandal.

The smell of leather, lemons and garlic filled the air, and I couldn't believe I was actually seeing the same makeshift dressing room with the same creepy salesman.

As soon as I spotted him, I looked at Lorenzo with surprise and we started laughing, saying, "Skivatz!" I gripped Lorenzo's hand tighter with fear and excitement as we inched closer. The smell of the street now mixed with the sweet florals coming from his store. He escorted me in first and his family was all there waiting for me with smiles.

They were all so beautiful and elegantly dressed. Of course, they all smelled amazing. They were visibly happy to see us and their huge smiles really broke the ice.

We kissed the traditional cheek kiss and exchanged pleasantries. His parents, sister and brother led the way to lunch at one of my favorite restaurants, La Lanterna. It was a beautiful reunion and the owner immediately recognized me.

He reached out to hug me while saying, "L'americana, L'americana, L'americana."

I guess he couldn't forget L'americana, who loved his pizza, little fried fish and homemade limoncello. Immediately, we had wine and food at our table. All kinds of vegetables and, of course, my little fried fish. Next came the buffalo mozzarella pizza with perfectly thin crust. I was in heaven and the owner was so good at cutting the tension.

He knew Lorenzo was previously married and that his mother was not a fan of mine.

He hid his shock at seeing us together and instead greeted me like his long-lost friend. We eased into conversation, especially with his brother and sister, helping to dissipate the tension.

We had great times together and for all of us, those were our 2 favorite summers growing up. Now everyone is healthy and happy and married with kids. They seemed genuinely happy to see me, because they knew it made their brother happy and that's all they really wanted. His father was the most jolly, happy and a warm fuzzy kind of man.

Everyone loved him, like they loved Lorenzo. He was definitely his father's son. His mother had eyes of steel. She was pleasant, but definitely wasn't overly warm. I'm hoping she's feeling the guilt of stealing my letters and keeping them from Lorenzo. If we're meant to be together, nothing can stop that from happening now. Not even her, and she knew it.

Every time his mother would ask me a question, Lorenzo would squeeze my leg as if he knew what she was doing and that I shouldn't worry. I'm sure she gave him an earful when he told her I was back in Italy. I would have loved to be a fly on the wall for that conversation. She asked how long I was staying in Italy and what I was writing about and my future plans.

Here we go!

I told her exactly what was going on and that I don't know what the future holds, but I'm open to anything. I hope she caught on that I was open to moving to Italy permanently, so she didn't have to worry about losing her son.

While drinking our limoncello, she asked if we were coming over for dinner and Lorenzo said we already had plans. I didn't know what to say since we didn't have plans, but his mother asked what they were.

"It's a surprise," Lorenzo said.

His mother raised an eyebrow.

"Ok, let's toast." I said, raising my glass to toast, trying to keep things light. Lunch went well and the food here is always amazing.

After an hour, we said our goodbyes because none of us were sure if we'd see each other again since my trip was so short and I actually had work to do. I told them I hoped we would meet at least once more. When it came time to say goodbye to his mother, she kissed my cheek and said, "Welcome home."

"Thank-you," I replied and squeezed her hands before letting go.

On the inside, I was dying. Is that her way of calling a truce? Is this her way of telling me I better move to Italy if I want her blessing to be with her son? I was happy, but also scared of her.

I was hoping this wasn't a cryptic message either. Women, and especially Italian mothers, can be very cryptic when it comes to getting their way and even more so when it involves their son.

After parting, I immediately told Lorenzo what his mother said and asked if that was a good thing or not. His eyes got big. He was surprised and asked me to repeat exactly what she said.

"Oh my god, Lorenzo, is this good or bad?" I asked.

"This is-a good, Ella. Very, very-a good," He responded.

I could see the wheels turning in his head of all the potential scenarios of us being together and how it could work now that he had his mother's blessing. Or maybe that was what I was thinking.

"My mother would-a never welcome someone unless-a she meant it, as you know," he said.

He grabbed my hand and led me through the Sorrento crowds back to the hotel room for dessert.

Lemon Mare

"No, I can never have too many lemon soaps from Positano. Leave me alone and just let me shop. Six months from now when the joy starts to fade, one sniff of these soaps and I'm happy again." - Lora Condon

The Grand Hotel Excelsior Vittoria really is grand. It is set back a bit from the street and has wrought-iron gates and shrubs to make it look very mysterious, elegant and secluded. Plants and trees are all around and it looks like you're entering royal gardens. I felt so lucky, special, and blessed to walk through the gate and wave to the guard.

He knew who I was, but when he saw me with Lorenzo, his face lit up and from then on he treated me like a long-lost friend every time I came and went.

They have 150 years of luxury hospitality experience and it shows. They curated every detail to showcase the beauty of the area and I was in heaven enjoying such luxury. Most of the hotel is made to view the bay that makes every meal a spectacle with a view of Vesuvio.

They have a Michelin chef who can draw from the hotel's curated orange grove. That's one way to get fresh, organic orange juice. Even though we just ate, we had to get a drink and relax at the Terrazza Vittoria bar looking out to Mount Vesuvius. I wish I could tattoo this on the inside of my eyelids so when I closed my eyes, I could still see the view. The bar area is gorgeous and let's face it, there's always room for a refreshing drink called Lemon

Mare.

I was lucky enough to have a hot guy named Luca step in to make our drinks. I felt like a princess being served by these two beautiful men. We had homemade limoncello, lemon juice from their garden, mint, Spanish gin and a slice of lemon to top it off. It was perfect in this heat. It was fun to watch the girls fawn over Luca. He was a gorgeous charmer for sure, and the ladies loved him.

We got another round of drinks and headed back to the room to sit on the balcony. The view is like a magnet that keeps pulling you back. It's almost impossible to leave, and the power of the pull is too much to fight. While looking out at the boats floating through the bay, Enzo pulled my hair back to one side and started kissing my neck so lightly that the heat from his breath and the breeze from the water gave me goosebumps all over and made me shake.

He then took the lemon from his drink and dragged it from my ear and down my neck, following it with kisses. I was melting. Once he got closer to my shoulder, he tugged on my shirt and kissed the inner part of my shoulder where there is a little indentation. There was nothing I could do but fall back into his chest and give into him. The lemon found its way to my collarbone. Starting from my right side, then to my left. Every inch was followed by his lips and tongue. He made his way across my collarbone and stopped in between my breasts. His lips and tongue followed the lemon as it slid all over my body.

Further and further down he went, kissing me without missing an inch. Up went my skirt as his head went under. I had to grip the balcony's edge to stop myself from losing balance and falling over. Eventually, he came back up and then slid behind me. He bent me over the balcony railing and had his way with me, not caring who could see us from their balcony, the street, roof or their boat. There was no stopping us and now I was one of the crazy Italians having sex in public, yet again. It's an epidemic here and now I was contributing to it.

If you're in Italy long enough, I guess it's only a matter of time before you're having sex in public. Oh well, the landscapers got a little more than they bargained for this afternoon! He knows how to push my buttons and so much more. I can't say "No." We then collapsed onto the bed to finish what we started and to build up an appetite for dinner. We napped for a while and then got ready for dinner. He said he had another surprise for me to help with my article. I can't take anymore surprises.

This was such a whirlwind, and my heart was literally bursting and overflowing with joy and love.

We hopped in the car to get some dinner and inspiration. I needed to focus on the songs that Italian Americans love, so I could show them the story behind the song. I felt this would be a great hook for readers to deepen their love for their favorite songs, coming mostly from the town of Naples in the Campania region. This is the region so many Italian Americans hail from, so it only makes sense. I also wanted readers to learn the English translation behind the great songs like "Arrivaderci Roma," "Volare," "Santa Lucia," "Core 'ngrato" and many more.

All the opera singers have sung these classic songs and many times Americans don't know the translation or the story behind the song and singer. I thought that would make for an interesting article and it was turning out better than expected. One way or another, I was going to write something worthy of Billboard Magazine.

For inspiration, we drove along the edge of the Sorrento Peninsula and up to Positano and walked around. Positano is so unique and I have beautiful memories there with Lorenzo and the Volpes.

John Steinbeck wrote about Positano saying, "It is a dream place that isn't quite real when you are there and becomes beckoningly real after you have gone." This is an incredibly accurate explanation of Positano.

Fried Fanuke

"I'd like a double plate of these, per favore." - Lora Condon

We parked right above Hotel Pupetto and walked down a few hundred steps to the beach. The approximate 300 steps down to the beach from the top of Hotel Pupetto can be brutal when it's hot. Thankfully, there was a little breeze. I loved this hotel, and I felt very European going there. The beach is great, and I felt so fancy having the chairs set up by the hotel attendants.

Those guys hustled to make your day enjoyable. It was a great beach to visit to feel like you're on vacation. No one ever set up my chairs down the shore in New Jersey. This hotel and beach made me feel like I was away from it all. It had a very different feeling than Punta Massa or the Jersey shore.

Positano is luxurious and you can't help but feel as if you're one of the most special and luckiest people in the world to be there… and you are! Even if you're not rich, you feel rich there. It's in the air.

Lorenzo already had this dinner planned out because when we arrived, the waiter brought us to a table right on the edge of the restaurant, facing the setting sun, with a bottle of red wine from Ischia waiting for us. This was so sweet and before I knew it, a huge plate of fried *finocchio* (fennel) arrived. The taste of warm licorice in a subtle fry was the Italian version of comfort food.

I can't believe he remembered my favorite dish from this restaurant. It seems like he remembers everything we did. It felt as if it was only last summer and nothing had changed. I think he had as much fun surprising me and seeing my reaction as I did getting surprised. He's not normal, I thought to myself. What man remembers these insignificant details? He was making it impossible to work and think about writing anything other than love notes.

"Ok Lorenzo, I have to actually work and get the information for this article before I leave. All I've done so far is eat, drink and have sex.

If that is what my article was about, it would be done by now, but it's not." He laughed, raised his glass to toast, and put his other arm around me. With the most confident, sexy, relaxed and suave voice, he said,

"But Mariella, that IS what Italy is all about. What could be better than this?"

He was so right; this is life. Here is a real life worth living with all the possibilities. Italians know how to live and live well. Americans make it so much more complicated than necessary. Our food is poison and killing us. People are more and more shallow every day and only living for social media "likes." Everyone is so angry and polarized to the extreme. As far as I'm concerned, everyone needs to sit down with a bottle of wine and watch the sunset every night. The world would be a much better place.

Lorenzo was almost successful in convincing me to relax, but I also had my mother on my shoulder with the wooden spoon in one hand and smacking it into her other hand, waiting to review my article.

"Ok, Lorenzo, what kind of information do you have for me about the stories behind the songs and singers? I have to do some writing on this trip," I pleaded.

Suddenly, the manager of the hotel came to the table to greet us. He always used to make sure to keep some extra fried *finocchio* for me during the summer, because he knew I would always make a double order, especially after an afternoon of drinking, swimming and boating. When a double order of fried *finocchio* came through the kitchen tonight, he knew it had to be me.

He came running out to see who ordered this dish. I was greeted with a huge hug and he couldn't believe *L'americana* was back and especially with Lorenzo.

Some Italian Americans called *finocchio, fanuke*. Everyone got a kick out of my crazy American-Italian words and the manager yelled,

"Fried *fanuke*, fried *fanuke*. Oh, how I miss hearing that. You and your *fanuke*! Ciao bella."

Let the party begin. Out came the Prosecco, cheeses, meats, and the Cuban cigars. He was always so proud that he could get Cuban cigars in Italy and we couldn't in America. We drank, we ate, we smoked, we laughed and reminisced. Positano perfection.

I figured the owner must know someone to help me with the article and sure enough; he did. Yes, I'm finally getting somewhere. Luckily, his friend Giuseppe runs one of the most historic opera houses on the Amalfi Coast, and he's on his way over from the main beach.

One of the coolest things about Hotel Pupetto is that if you walk along the coastline from the hotel and around the mountain, you'll end up right at the main beach and dock of Positano.

That's what makes this the perfect hotel. You're a 10-minute walk to the heart of the city with ferries to Capri or Ischia, but away from the crowds and cruise boat tourists. The floors in the lobby are blue and white tiles, typical of the Sorrento Peninsula.

Just looking at them calms me.

A few minutes later, Giuseppe came walking into the restaurant from the mountain walkway and when he spotted the manager, he came right over to our table. After the introductions and kisses, Giuseppe said he would love to help me because he could talk opera all day long. His family owned that opera house for generations, so they knew almost everyone and lots of juicy behind-the-scenes gossip you can't Google. Fantastic!

I took out my pad and asked him a few questions before we had to head out to downtown Positano for the rest of my surprise.

My first question was about my favorite opera song, "Core 'ngrato," meaning Ungrateful Heart. The version I prefer is sung by half-Neopolitan, Sergio Franchi, the Italian opera singer who moved to America. The music was written in 1911 by Salvatore Cardillo and the lyrics were by Riccardo Cordiffero. This Neopolitan style song was written by an Italian who moved to America, so it was only right that this was one of Sergio's signature songs.

The first words of the song are *Catari*, which is short for Caterina. The chorus talks about an ungrateful heart who has ruined his life and she never even thinks about him.

It's a very dramatic song and you don't even need to know the words because you can feel the pain of the jilted lover as the song crescendos.

Only the most skilled of singers can handle this masterpiece. I once asked a singer in a restaurant in Little Italy, New York, to sing this song and I swear he gave me the evil eye. He said it surprised him such a young girl would know this song. It's a song that true opera lovers adore because so few can sing it correctly.

Cordiffero was definitely a passionate man and a political activist in favor of more extreme socialism. He eventually moved to America and I have to wonder why he would have moved to a capitalistic country, but Giuseppe said, "He was a typical socialist that thinks spending everyone else's money is great as long as you don't spend his." He was even jailed for his speeches and radical writings. Cordiffero was also one of the writers to highlight the plight and exploitation of legal Italian immigrants in New York City in his piece titled *L'onore Perduto* or *Lost Honor*. Most Americans have no clue how Italian immigrants were discriminated against or even hung in America just for being Italian.

Today most people would think it was fake news.

"Core 'ngrato" was first sung by Enrico Caruso, followed by all the great tenors in history. I love Sergio Franchi's version best because he had a very robust voice and his emotions were not lost to classical training. Sergio was the typical, big-hearted, jovial, southern Italian.

He was happy, talented, and madly in love with his wife. I also have a special place in my heart for Sergio because when my sister was about 7 years old, my parents went to see Sergio sing and took her with them.

When they arrived at the New York nightclub, the person at the door tried to persuade them to not bring my sister because they were afraid she would misbehave, especially at a long show featuring opera and classic songs. My father assured her my sister would be well-behaved and the lady reluctantly let them in after he passed her some cold hard cash.

The hostess had no idea that my sister loved Sergio. She also had no idea what it was like to grow up with American-Italian parents. At any moment, we knew we could be smacked in the face or the back of the head or both: in public or at home. The rod, the belt, the wooden spoon, and the hand were never spared, and we completely understood this truth. All it took was a subtle look in case we forgot what was forthcoming should we misbehave. Sergio was so impressed with my sister. He took her up on stage, sang to her, took pictures and gave her his hat he wore during the show. It was a memory she would never forget, and I was always jealous that she had that experience.

Sergio was one of Ed Sullivan's favorite guests, granting him 24 appearances on his show. He was extremely talented and could cover comedy in addition to pure Italian drama. Unfortunately, he died in 1990. He was posthumously awarded the title of *Cavaliere* [Knight] in the Order of Merit (*Stella al merito del lavoro*) by the Italian Government for his support of the Boys' and Girls' Towns of Italy. He had a huge heart and his wife has carried on his passion for opera by hosting fundraising concerts, showcasing the newest and best opera talent at their home in Connecticut. As Giuseppe was telling me about Sergio, he mentioned the song "Moon Over Naples" that he recorded in 1965.

I knew the song, but really never thought about it. Lorenzo looked at me with a smirk and I asked him why he was smirking. He asked me if I knew the words and I said I didn't remember, so he pulled up the lyrics on his phone.

They were beautiful and romantic. I can hear Sergio singing about the moon over Naples and how his love promised to love him but left him and he asks the moon to shine it's light so he can find her. Totally dreamy.

I imagined Lorenzo waiting for me to return while looking out over the Bay of Naples like Enrico Caruso. We all had a moment of awkward silence and then I asked Giuseppe to tell me more.

I was in my glory and so grateful. I also realized I didn't have any Italian women featured. Unfortunately, the classics always seem to go to the men.

I had to ask about Cecelia Bartoli because she's one of the most famous modern Italian opera singers. Cecelia doesn't have the dramatic appeal of Maria Callas, which might be a good thing, but she's a major force in the opera world and has incredible sales to prove it. She is a coloratura mezzo-soprano and actually once lost a singing competition.

Obviously, she won later on and in a big way, with a captivating and popular role as Rosina, in *The Barber of Seville*.

Giuseppe told me that her voice is so perfect it almost isn't real. It's impossible to believe that someone can hit all those notes so quickly and so perfectly. She has mastered the most impossible pieces of music; a true master. Unfortunately, most Americans do not know her as well as the other singers of our era.

Maybe if she was popular for singing classic American Italian songs, she would be better known in America; but sadly, she is not. I feel like she missed the crooner generation in American and thus she's not as well known with the first and second generation Italian-Americans. She's one of a kind. I've always wanted to meet her since her smile electrifies a room. I have some crazy idea that we would be fast friends, going shopping and drinking Aperol Spritzes somewhere on the Amalfi Coast.

I couldn't wait to ask him about Renata Tebaldi. She is one of the women along with Maria Callas that I really enjoy. Growing up, I think the women I heard sing opera the most were these two women. Ironically, they had a rumored intense rivalry.

It's a silly rivalry because one woman can't sing every opera performance in the world at the same time. There is plenty of room for both and I find them both unique. Giuseppe said that in the 1950s, Maria Callas said Renata had no spine. Tebaldi retorted: "I have one thing that Callas doesn't have: a heart." Callas said that comparing her with Tebaldi was like "comparing Champagne with Cognac, No, Coca-Cola." Yikes! Good thing these women did not have social media.

Giuseppe believed some of the jealousy between the women resulted from Renata having an easier time coming up in the opera world than Callas. Some believe Callas needed the help of her wealthy husband to get ahead. She owns it and I don't care what any critic or competitor writes.

Either way, the world was blessed to have them both for so long. I believe no one can sing Habanero from Carmen like Callas.

I love the recordings of Renata with that 1940s Bugs Bunny, WWII soundtrack sound. It makes her voice more memorable. She's the voice of an era for me. Her version of "O Mio Babbino Caro" from one of Puccini's arias is gorgeous. She was also the voice behind Sophia Loren's role in *Aida* in 1953. Talk about two powerful women coming together.

Surprisingly, Renata had polio as a child and because she wasn't allowed to do any strenuous activity, she took up singing and piano. It probably saved her life and healed her mind, body and soul. She sang professionally for over 30 years and sacrificed having a marriage and family to focus on her career.

She mentioned she had an international family of fans and did not need to be married. Her mother and maid were her closest confidants and assistants. She was definitely a different type of woman for her time.

The information I was receiving was incredible and right before I was going to ask for more, Lorenzo squeezed my leg, put his hand on my jaw, and turned it towards him.

"Onto my next-a surprise-a my love" he said with a sweet kiss.

"Ok, I'm ready to see what you have in store next."

I grabbed his face and kissed him so loudly, we all laughed and the manager said, "Oh, I have missed you both so much. You were so happy and in love. What happened? I'm so glad you're back together like you should be.

This is happiness, this is amore. *Mi piace molto, i miei amici."* (I like it a lot, my friends).

We looked at each other with such love, but also some sadness for the lost years. Lorenzo replied to the owner, saying,

"You are right, *amico mio*, (my friend). I have never been a-happy since the day she left-a me. How do we keep-a her here and stop her from returning to America?"

The owner replied, "It is easy. Never leave her side."

All four of us looked at each other and agreed with our faces that, yes, that was a good idea and made perfect sense.

"Ok, *grazie. Andiamo, andiamo* [lets go]," Lorenzo said as he got up.

The men all exchanged pleasantries in Italian. I'm sure they told him to not let go of me this time. After thanking Giuseppe profusely and promising to meet up again, we said our goodbyes, and I promised to be back sooner rather than later.

We walked from Pupetto around the side of the mountain path that follows the ocean onto the grand beach of Positano.

We started walking up the town steps. Lorenzo blindfolded me, turned me around in circles, and led me up a pathway to the shops. He wouldn't tell me where we were and I couldn't imagine where we were going that I needed to be blindfolded.

This was so exciting and I could literally see in my mind the other tourists looking at me and thinking this guy was going to propose to me. I was pretty sure he didn't have a ring ready, or at least I was hoping he didn't. I don't know how we could pull off a relationship and I didn't want to ruin my real-life fantasy with reality just yet.

After a few minutes of walking, he took off my blindfold, and I was standing in the middle of one of my favorite stores with the staff standing there waiting for my expression. I was in shock. Here I was in the middle of the Mena Cinque Clothing Store.

It was here that they dressed me for many of my dates with Lorenzo. It was here I went to find the perfect outfit to meet his parents; where I went to find the dress to bring me into womanhood and where I went to find the best love counselors. I cherished the days I came here to buy the perfect outfit or accessory to make Lorenzo fall in love with me all over again. I also got the benefit of the wise advice from the women on how to proceed with a man like Lorenzo.

Never did I leave there not looking chic, fabulous and Italian. Not to mention confident, sexy and powerful. They taught this crazy in love college girl the art of seduction through clothes, mannerisms and playing it cool. Italian men were professional lovers and romancers. Jersey boys were nothing like this and couldn't care less about romance or love.

I had no guidelines or teachings on how to deal with Italian men, but these ladies took me under their wing and taught me how to play hard to get. I learned to never show all my cards and to keep him guessing. Lorenzo was a pro, and I clearly was not. I was lucky that these ladies knew him and approved. They also knew his mother was the nut I would have to crack. They were not able to offer much hope there.

As soon as I opened my eyes and realized where I was, we all opened our arms and had a group hug. Oh, how I missed them. They were my private cheerleaders and suddenly I felt like I was that nieve girl again who knew nothing of the big, bad world.

Lorenzo knew they dressed me for all the important occasions, but he had no idea that these women pretty much knew everything about him and I. They loved me, loved him and most of all, they loved us together. We reminisced about all the amazing outfits they had and some of the special events that happened in each outfit.

Then the owner said, "Remember that lovely tight white lace dress with the shimmer woven through it?"

"Oh, I loved that dress so much," Lorenzo added, and then said, "I remember that dress-a very well. I remember mmm, how it looked on your body and how-a much I loved that-a dress. I like it even more-a in a ball on the beach."

We all laughed, and even after all these years, I still blushed. When I was going out that night with Lorenzo, they made sure I had *the* dress that he would remember forever, and now we know he did.

We had a good laugh and then out came the limoncello to toast and celebrate our reunion. They were as close as family as far as I was concerned. It felt like yesterday, but I also ached for the missed years.

They wouldn't let me leave without giving me a dress. How could I refuse? She told me to choose anything in the store I wanted, but what I really wanted was for them to pick a dress to start the next part of my life. They all agreed that Lorenzo should pick out an outfit for me. His eyes got big, and he was so excited to be a part of dressing his very own Ella doll. Being an Italian man who was well-groomed and exposed to the most elegant people around, he had exquisite taste.

He said he was going to choose a dress for our last night and that it was going to be a surprise. He made me leave with a saleswomen to get a gelato down the hill while he bought me something special.

When I returned, he had the biggest smile, and they all stood staring at me. It was so awkward and I didn't know what to do with myself. I felt so special. We all hugged goodbye and told them I would try to stop by before returning to America.

They looked shocked when I told them I was not staying in Italy. I told them I wanted to stay, but my assignment was for only a few weeks. They made faces as if I was making excuses and I guess I was, but only in my fantasies did I believe I'd end up staying in Italy with Lorenzo. I never thought through the details and reality of moving to Italy.

I reassured them I would try to find a way to come back as soon as possible and I wasn't lying. They were happy with that answer, but didn't believe me. They looked at Lorenzo as if they felt bad that I was leaving him again. I know they were wondering how he could let me go. We finally said our goodbyes and Lorenzo made sure to send up a bunch of bottles of fabulous fragrance the next day as a thank you.

Little Pink Lights

"When we plan a menu, we try to emulate the harmony and flow of great music. If it all works together - color, texture, flavor, aroma - the enjoyment factor increases exponentially and makes a lasting impression." Dee Dee Sorvino speaking about her and her husband Paul Sorvino and how they love to entertain.

Mostly all I think about is food. After sharing my fried "fanuke" earlier, I was ready to eat. All this excitement got me hungry. Well, then again, just being in Italy makes me hungry. We're losing valuable eating time and the gelato didn't cut it. I needed some serious carbs. We walked up a ton of steps and hopped on a Vespa that was at the top of the hill and very well planned. Enzo drove me around to a very familiar hotel. Il San Pietro di Positano is one of the most spectacular hotels in the world.

Lorenzo and I used to come here and party with the owners on their private beach, private yacht and private everything! Many of the business owners that cater to the tourists between Sorrento and Positano know each other and spend a lot of their free time together while their kids all hang out. They all watch out for each other and basically barter their goods, services, time, and food. It's a beautiful, unofficial club in which to belong. It gives you access to the best that the Amalfi Coast has to offer and for someone like me, it's good to be a friend of a friend and even better to be the girlfriend or wife.

During those summers, people were a little surprised to see

Lorenzo with a very average girl like me, because of his status and good looks. They knew that there must be something very special or different about me that Lorenzo would forgo the hot bimbos.

He barely dated during the time we were apart those two years. His heart was with me, and this made people take note of me. It created such a buzz at the start of my second summer, it automatically put me onto Southern Italy's unofficial most wanted woman list. It was a long list of amazing, gorgeous, wealthy, smart socialites from the area like the Nivea girl. Being wanted by someone that everyone wanted landed me on that list.

I was the seemingly average American and now the unicorn they all wanted. They would trip over themselves to get a glimpse of me, to see what all the fuss was about. Lorenzo and I laughed about it, especially since I had no idea who he was when I met him and the whole socialite thing. The fact that I didn't care made him love me even more. It wasn't me that was so different or special; it was Lorenzo. He differed from the rest of them.

He wanted a real soul connection and was willing to wait for it. Enzo wasn't into having as many girls as possible; which goes against the stereotypical Italian male philosophy. Just like you can't have one potato chip, you can't have one woman. A lot of the girls disliked me and were actually mean, but I didn't care. I thought the whole thing was stupid and so my circle of female friends was small. My female friends tended to be older women, too old for Lorenzo, who saw the silly desperation of the young girls or girls in very committed relationships. Those older women like the women in the Cinque store. helped to explain the Italian socialite rules, expectations and way of life.

The San Pietro was the ultimate in socialite living. This hotel was known for elegance, class and incredible beauty. It's a special place that never leaves your heart and memory.

We used to come here a lot to eat, look fabulous and to have sex down at the private beach cove. I'm not sure how private it actually was, but we did what we had to do. I became one of those crazy Italians, having sex outside in the not-so-private area.

While walking through the hotel, I was greeted by people I used to go boating and shopping with years ago. "Ella, Ella, Ella," I heard from all over the hotel lobby. Such wonderful and great memories. I was so angry at myself for not returning sooner.

What was I thinking? This could have been my life all along. Although everyone said their hellos along the way, they also left us just as quickly, which was strange. I couldn't figure out why everyone left us. I figured they were busy working, but it didn't seem that busy that they couldn't stay and talk more. As we got further down the garden path, it got darker, more quiet and secluded. Then I saw little pink lights strung through the trees with a table set for two. As soon as I realized this whole area was for us, I stopped walking and started crying a little. Lorenzo watched me take it all in.

He was actually afraid that I wasn't happy, and that it wasn't good enough. I had to reassure him this was magnificent and way over the top. I had to hug him and thank him profusely. He said, "Anything for you, my libelulla bella." I believed him. I knew right then and there I could ask him for anything and he would give it to me or do it for me.

I knew he would give me his heart forever. Who knew when he had all this extra time to coordinate a day like today? The fact that he remembered all of my favorite things and was pulling out the stops to make my time in Italy unforgettable was special. Honestly, he didn't have to do anything and I still would have had the best time being in Italy with the man I love.

We walked closer to the table and Prosecco, meats and cheeses were waiting for us. It was the most romantic table under the stars. The little pink lights gave his face the most beautiful glow. I hoped it did the same for mine. Our table was at the very end of the hotel property. The view from the top of the cliff down to the private beach and the Mediterranean Sea was grand and majestic. Before we sat down, we got our glasses of Prosecco and stood at the very edge of the cliff.

We looked out at the cruise ship lights and billionaire yachts twinkling like diamonds on the sea. Lorenzo turned towards me to clink our glasses. He took a deep breath and looked me right in the eyes. All I could think of was that he was going to propose. Would he really do this? It would make sense after going through all this effort for one night. If he gets down on one knee, I'll die. I'm overwhelmed even thinking about how this relationship could work.

He put his hand on my cheek with his fingers behind my ear and then moved his thumb towards my lips and sang, "Darling, you look wonderful tonight."

I felt like I was glowing and glistening under these little pink lights. My lashes still had some teardrops on them. I could see them mixed with the pink light coming through my lashes. It was magical.

He then moved closer and put his hand around my waist and we started to slow dance. Rocking back and forth as he kind of hummed and sang both of Ed Sheeren's and Andrea Bocelli's verses in their romantic song. He then kissed me with the most gentle of kisses on my lips.

Then he turned slightly towards the water and said my name. I suddenly thought to myself, "Oh God, here it comes. He's gonna propose."

He continued, while pointing to the ocean, "My beautiful Mariella, as we look out into-a eternity or rather-a infinity, I see-a no limits. My love-a for you has-a no limits and our-a love-a knows, no limits.

When I gave you that-a infinity perfume-a years ago, I knew you were-a the one. Everyone in the Amalfi Coast knew you were-a the one for me. I almost married, but it was not-a love and everyone knew. It was-a for business and for-a show and my mamma. Definitely not-a love. You are-a my only *amore, cara mia* [love, my dear]. I want you to-a know that-a I never want -a to be-a without-a you ever again."

My mind started racing. What exactly does this mean and how does this play out in reality? How can we ever be together? Immediately, a look came over my face that must have looked like doubt and worry, because his face changed from serious and happy to serious and sad.

"What's the problemma, Mariella?"

"Nothing, Lorenzo. I love you so much, but I don't know how to make it work. How can this work?" I asked in a pleading voice for some reasonable response to calm my fears.

"My beautiful dragonfly, you are always such-a the worrier. Have you not learned anything in Italia? It will happen. We are meant-a to be together. You think and-a worry too much." He leaned in closer to my face.

I took a deep breath and said, "How are you so sure? You are talking like we don't live on different continents. You're so calm and confident, like you can throw up a prayer and it will happen."

Lorenzo backed up a little, got a very stern look on his face and looked me dead in the eye like I never saw before and said, "I never told you this but-a when you left-a me and never returned, I was-a dead, no passion. *Mi famiglia* [my family] sent-a me to San Giovanni Rotondo to meet with the priests and spiritual directors at San Pio's church. I stayed there for a few months and the priests helped me become a spiritual child of Padre Pio. I asked Pio and the priests to pray and intercede for me. If-a God ever sent you back-a to me, I would-a not be angry you left. I would-a never let you go again and do everything under-a God to be together forever. So here I am-a, living my promise to God.

When-a you wrote to me saying you were writing about Padre Pio and wanted to go to-a San Giovanni Rotondo, it was like a direct-a sign from San Pio that he orchestrated all of this. It set me on fire and felt like an answered prayer. I couldn't believe it."

I gushed, "Oh, Lorenzo, I had no idea. I feel awful now. I'm so sorry. I swear, I had no idea you felt like this."

I had to hold him as he fell into my arms, heavy, like all the prayers of the last years fell off of him. We stood silent to let all the pain leave our bodies. When we separated, we both felt free and lighter.

We smiled at each other under the lights. I couldn't argue with Padre Pio. That definitely stopped me in my tracks and reminded me of his famous quote, "Pray, hope, and don't worry." Sounds like good advice to me.

We went back to the table to eat some cheese and meat with grapes. We sat next to each other in order to look out over the endless ocean. Lorenzo told me that the day before I emailed him, one priest he knew from San Giovanni Rotondo called him.

 The priest said that Padre Pio came to him in his dream and told him to call the young boy Lorenzo from Sorrento, that stayed in San Giovanni Rotondo. Padre Pio told him that his prayers will soon be answered. Lorenzo mentioned he hadn't talked to the priests there in a few years because it was too painful. They would send Christmas cards, but nothing too deep. Lorenzo didn't even let them know I was in Italy. He wanted to surprise the priests when we got there. Enzo couldn't believe I was writing about Padre Pio and it freaked him out because he knew I was not aware he spent time in San Giovanni Rotondo. This will be a true miracle if we end up together, I thought.

The manager came over with a bottle of wine already picked by Lorenzo. It was a red, dark, heavy, bold wine from Ischia and, most of all, smooth going down. When the manager returned, he came with a waiter bringing about 10 plates of food for this hungry army of two, consisting of *frutta di mare*, [fish salad] pasta, and fresh vegetables from their garden.

We asked the manager to have some wine with us to celebrate my return to Italy, so he sat and reminisced over the good ole days. They work very hard at this hotel and even have a Michelin chef. The San Pietro hotel is the standard of excellence and they have mastered the art of service. The fact that someone this busy made the time to sit and have a glass of wine with us was such an honor. He described each dish with pride and precision. Many of the ingredients we were eating were actually grown right here in this garden.

The fennel and parsley burst when chewed, causing an explosion of flavor igniting my senses. Eating in Italy definitely takes over all of your senses.

I had to ask him about any opera singers that frequented this hotel. He assured me that all the great Italian opera singers and many celebrities have stayed here since the hotel opened.

The private beach ensures privacy as well as exclusivity. Everyone at the hotel's beach cove is looking for privacy and no paparazzi. It is very easy for them to take a boat right up to the beach, so no one sees them coming in from the front door or the street. I can also attest to the fact that it was also a nice beach for wild affairs. If those stone walls of the caves could only talk. The manager soon left us to continue our conversation and eat "under the romance" as he said with a devilish smile.

When the chocolate dessert and homemade limoncello made from the lemons in their garden arrived, I was in a state of bliss. Can life get any better? The sweetness of the chocolate with the tart citrus created a wonderful balance that was quite refreshing and light.

I can't even believe this is my life, considering a week ago I was praying to Jesus, Mary and Padre Pio to be right here. I figured one of them had to be listening to me beg and plead. While standing there, I thought about becoming a spiritual child of Padre Pio as well.

Can we ever have enough prayer covering us or people interceding for us?

I didn't want to leave this setting, but Lorenzo took my hand and led me down the elevator built in the stone wall to go down to the beach. It was very dark with no one in the cove. It was like our own private beach. The waves were so loud crashing against the cliff we couldn't hear anything or anyone. That made it the perfect place to be alone. Enzo and I walked to the water, which was nice and warm.

He slowly started kissing my neck and cleverly unzipped my dress without me really even noticing, because his hands were moving all over my back. He was a pro! Before I knew it, his pants were off and we were naked and jumping in the water. It was so refreshing after being out all day long.

I miss the days of such carefree living when it was fun with no thoughts of the future. Now, it seemed as if every move I made had consequences. Every move felt like I was in a living chess game. Part of me felt like I was young again and the other half was filled with worry, fear and anxiety about what would happen between us and the future after I leave.

While running 1,000 different scenarios in my head, Enzo swam up behind me and asked if I wanted to recreate the last time we were here at night.

"Yes, let's recreate it and make it even better," I said. His green eyes lit up and sparkled from the moonbeams reflecting off of them. His teeth glowed as he smiled a big smile as he asked what

I had in mind to make it better. I said, "this" and I took a deep breath and went down under the water.

Uncle Funzie

"It's what happens when you're really young; you want to feel different and be part of the new wave. Music helps you do that. It becomes so much more than just music —it helps to create your identity." Jovanotti

The next morning, Lorenzo had to leave early for work, which was fine because I was determined to do a lot of research and finish as much of my article as possible. I also had to call my mother. I was dreading the 10,000 question game. Up until now, I was texting her to let her know I was ok and Lorenzo was taking care of me.

Soon, I would have to call and start answering some hard questions. First, I need a cappuccino and carbs before I dealt with that conversation. Although I considered having my breakfast brought up in the Caruso suite, I figured I should hang out at the hotel restaurant to see if I could make some connections.

The clientele at this hotel are always interesting. Someone must have some good opera gossip they're dying to tell me.

It was a glorious day outside. I love Sorrento an hour or two right before the height and heat of the sun. It is warm, but still has that gentle, cool breeze that tricks you into thinking you won't need that much SPF. You forget it and then burn the rest of the day. Thanks to the Nivea girl, I never had a sunburn again.

I love Italian hotel breakfasts. It usually consists of vegetables grown right in their garden, like tomatoes, cucumbers, peppers, and arugula. They couple that with fresh mozzarella, homemade ricotta, and some other cheeses matched with meats. There is no way to not finish that off with a wonderfully flaky, fresh pastry and some more cappuccino. I picked a table all the way at the end of the outdoor seating so I could have some peace, but also to sit and stare at the ocean. I love watching the boats going in and out of the gulf. The sun dancing on the water like diamonds is mesmerizing, and every time I see it, it's like the first time seeing such beauty.

Sitting alone with my nose in my laptap pretty much means don't bother me. Don't you know some guy had to sit at the table right next to me, even though there were many available tables in the outside section. This reminds me of when you go to the Jersey shore. No one else is at the beach, but loud people will sit within 5 feet of where you put your blanket. It's mind-blowing and makes my head explode. Then I thought of Padre Pio and I felt guilty for wanting to put my fork in the guy's eyeballs and flick them over the cliff.

I thought maybe God was testing me to see how much of an open heart I have to share with the world. "Ok, God. You win. I'll talk to him and be nice."

The other diner kept making eye contact with me. Finally, I introduced myself and did the usual pleasantries. His name was Funzi and told me everyone calls him Uncle Funzie. He asked what I was writing about and I told him about my article on opera and Padre Pio. He seemed interested and asked me if I had completed my research and I told him, "I only have half of what I need done. I reunited with an old friend and he's been distracting me. We've been eating and drinking and hitting the beach."

"Yes, Italy has a way to distract and lure you into her, so you will forgo all else," he said.

I was surprised how well he expressed my feelings. I asked him what he did for a living and he replied he was a retired opera singer and had a lot of good stories to share if I was interested. Yes, I want! He joked, saying he wasn't famous, but he has performed in many opera houses around the world with the greats.

He still does a little musical theater around the world when the spirit moves him. Now he prefers teaching voice and mentoring. This is a total score for me. I mentioned to him I'm staying in the Caruso suite and I saw a little twinkle in his eye. "If you give me some great stories behind the songs, I'll show you the suite," I promised.

"Si, si, molto bene," he responded.

"Well, I haven't written about Pavarotti yet. I mean, how do you write only a little bit about the greatest and most famous opera singer the world has ever seen? He's basically the Babe Ruth of opera.

He's the one singer everyone knows around the world no matter what, so I'm having trouble figuring out how to fit him in without totally taking over all the other singers. Any suggestions?" I pleaded.

"Pavarotti," he said, "was a very complex man and there was no way any man could live up to his own legend. He came close, but all men have a major flaw. That is also what makes us love him so much. We all have major flaws, but ours are not on the front page of the newspaper."

I couldn't argue. I needed information about any of the songs he sang that had interesting stories behind them or anything that would be book worthy.

Uncle Funzie and I were having a great conversation, and I told him my father's favorite opera singers were Mario Lanza, Sergio Franchi and Luciano Pavarotti. All three were very different and great in their own style. I'll never forget waking up late at night while my father would be drinking wine, shining his shoes and playing opera records in the living room.

Old Italian men love shining their shoes. It was one of his favorite things to do! My favorite album cover was Pavarotti's Greatest Hits album, where he was dressed like a clown beating a drum. I think my father wore that album out. Later, I learned it was Pagliacci, not a clown.

In addition to his incredible opera house career, in 1990, his version of "Nessun Dorma" [Let No One Sleep], from Puccini's opera, *Turandot*, was the official song of the World Cup. He had such class and elegance. I don't see an opera song ever being the World Cup anthem again, but one never knows.

His performance at the World Cup took this song out of the opera houses and into the people's houses. It was the modern-day explosion of opera to the people who would never listen to opera.

Uncle Funzie also told me that some of Pavarotti's canceled performances were never going to happen. I was shocked. He said that Pavarotti was too ill to perform, but people wanted to keep his name and sales relevant, so they would book a performance, promote it and it would never happen. How sad for everyone involved except those making royalties off of record sales.

I asked him about the song "O Sole e Mio," which many associate with Pavarotti. He told me it was written by a Neapolitan composer, Eduardo di Capua. I wondered to myself why so much talent has come out of Naples and the surrounding area. Eduardo also wrote one of my favorite songs, "Marie, Ah Marie," which is a lot less well-known.

That catchy song is about a woman doing laundry on a beautiful, sunny day. It goes to show that everything is better in Italy and in Italian.

Pavarotti's big debut was Puccini's, *La Boheme* in 1961. That same opera also launched Mario Lanza's career around 1949. Interestingly enough, Pavarotti used to watch Mario Lanza movies and then go home and imitate Lanza in the mirror. Imagine being the singer that inspired Pavarotti! It's a classic opera, but given Pavarotti's ability to effortlessly hit the high C, he is often considered the ultimate tenor. When the great tenor, Enrico Caruso sang the aria, "Che Gelida Manina", from La Boheme, Puccini said to him, "Who sent you to me, God?"

Personally, I think Lanza was a little smoother than Pavarotti and would have been just as famous if he didn't die so young at the age of thirty-eight. Uncle Funzie actually agreed with me. Lanza was a heavy drinker, overeater and also took unregulated prescribed drugs to lose weight. He would even use the controversial therapy of sleep deprivation to lose weight.

Doctors believe these extremes caused his heart to eventually give out. Like any great drama, the truth is only known to a few people. It was a substantial loss to the opera world and his family as well as mine.

Caruso

"I suffer so much in this life. That is what they [the audience] are feeling when I sing, that is why they cry. People who felt nothing in this life cannot sing." - Enrico Caruso

With all this great information, I led Uncle Funzi up to the Caruso suite. The staff at the hotel knew who he was, so they all made a point to stop and greet him. A few of the staff actually came up with us to the suite to discuss the history and tell some legendary stories to add to my article. This was all a writer's dream. It's a special room and not because it's a large suite but because you can feel the history. Even walking down the hallway to the room is beautiful. When you enter room 448, it's like being transported back to 1921.

Exquisite wallpaper covers the walls. They filled antique furniture with books and artifacts. Pictures of Enrico Caruso grace the walls, along with a caricature of Caruso drawn by Caruso himself. A glorious desk faces the window and I can only imagine Enrico sitting there writing poetry, music and going over operas he would sing. There is also his original piano, which is the highlight of the room for any musician or opera lover. In the bathroom, marble frames the claw bathtub, which of course is fit for a king.

The balcony view of Vesuvio is spectacular. Every view of Vesuvio is sweet and special. I can only imagine how Caruso felt staying in this room as he reminisced on his life's path to

Sorrento and the world. His mother died when he was young, so he took to singing in the streets of Naples to make money for the family and then graduated to singing in resorts.

With the money he made from the resorts, he bought his first pair of new shoes. In 1896, his career was growing and he actually wore a bedspread like a toga for one of his publicity pictures.

Unfortunately, it was not a publicity stunt. He didn't have a clean shirt to wear while he was waiting for the only shirt he owned to be cleaned.

I made a point to get Uncle Funzie's information to send him a copy of my article and use him as a reference if I needed more information. After such a productive morning, I was ready to take a nap.

We parted ways, and I took one of the balcony chairs from my room, laid it flat and took a nice nap under the sun. I snoozed with kisses from the ocean breeze.

I felt someone's lips on mine and I was happy to see it was Lorenzo, not Uncle Funzie. He joined me on the lounge and we napped for a bit under the beautiful weather.

"So, what are we doing for one of our last nights in Sorrento?" I quietly asked as I bounced between the conscious and unconscious.

Enzo brushed the hair from my face and said, "*Vongole* [baby clams]." I looked at him, confused, and then my face lit up and a big smile came across my face. I knew this meant we were going to another one of my favorite restaurants, La Conca in Meta owned by the famous Antonio.

"Yes, La Conca, *andiamo subito*, (hurry up, let's go] for the sunset," I said.

"Yes, Mariella, *subito*; right after I have my way with you." He grabbed my hands, pulled me up, and carried me off the balcony into the room and onto the bed. "Let's work for our hunger, yes?" he said, as he kissed my ankles and worked his way up.

"Yes, work Lorenzo, work," I screamed.

When we walked onto the deck where all the tables and chairs are at La Conca, the waiter greeted Lorenzo and introduced himself to me. He led us to our table right on the edge of the beach so we could watch the sunset with a bottle of wine. This was the only place to be to watch the sunset in peace and quiet before dinner.

As the sun was about to disappear and kiss us *arrivaderci* [goodbye], the owner came out to greet Lorenzo. As he was shaking Enzo's hand, his head turned to me and he was shocked. He couldn't believe it was me.

"Mariella, L'americana, I can't believe it, you are really here," he said loudly.

I stood up to give him a big hug. "I can't believe I'm here either," I said. We all laughed and I told him the story of how and why I am back in Italy and that soon we are headed to San Giovanni Rotundo to learn more about Padre Pio, for my article.

He looked at Lorenzo and asked him if he had been back there since the last time he was there. Lorenzo shook his head side to side, motioning no. Antonio got quiet and asked us to pray for him at the shrine because he also loves Padre Pio. We assured him we would and that I had a long list of people to pray for when I arrived.

The owner yelled to his waiter to get me a big bowl of *vongole* and then he rattled off a whole bunch of dishes he knew I would love. It was like I'd never left. Enjoying peaceful, happy times with beautiful souls, sitting together watching God's best artwork.

We all talked about opera and our favorite songs. I let him know what I had so far and it would be great if he had any more information for my article. He gave me a few unique stories from singers that had been to his restaurant and how the Sorrento Peninsula inspired so many singers, artists, writers and, of course, lovers.

As much as I loved the opera talk, the food kept distracting me. With every dish brought out, I had to take a moment of silence to appreciate a different genre of art. Food art, or as we now call it, "Food Porn." The *vongole* here can't be beat. Every clam is juicy and cooked to perfection. I don't even need the spaghetti. I can eat a whole dish of *vongole*. The tomatoes here remind me of the tomatoes we would grow as kids in Jersey. They're little balls of sweet, juicy love. They also picked a white wine from Ischia for my Italian, who matches his food with the wine and then a deep dark, dry red from Ischia for me. He remembered.

How lucky it is to be loved by Italians who own restaurants. They remember the details of their guests and can't wait to make you happy.

Real people pleasers in the truest form of love, friendship, and joy. I wish I had an extra week in order to eat here every night! The highlight of eating at this restaurant is putting your glass of wine on the bannister, above the shoreline, so it sits perfectly centered in the middle of the setting sun.

Even though every picture looked the same, we took hundreds of pictures, getting a time-lapse of the sun setting into the wineglass. Another night that was pure perfection.

The next day we mostly laid in bed while I worked on my article, made some phone calls and brushed Lorenzo's shiny curls from his eyes while he napped. I couldn't believe how in love we were and how gorgeous he still was after so many years.

Room service on the balcony, crisp Prosecco with lunch and Lorenzo for my afternoon break, was a life I could easily see myself living. While researching for my article, I found a restaurant on the water that looked very unique. I asked Lorenzo if he ever heard of Lo Scoglio in Massa Lubrense and of course he did and said it was one of his favorite places that he and his friends used to hang out at for dinner before clubbing. While reminiscing over his past escapades, his phone rang, and it was his mother. They talked for a bit and he told her we were going to Lo Scoglio for dinner. I could hear she was so happy and I found it very strange, but maybe she was softening up to me since I'm leaving in a few days. They hung up, and we got ready to go. I thought I was being paranoid, so I let it go.

Upon arrival at Lo Scoglio, I saw a huge, stone fish tank in the middle of the restaurant. All the fish came in fresh daily from the fishermen and you actually got to choose the fish you wanted to eat for dinner. Only in Italy!! As we were leaning over, checking out the night's fare, a woman came up to Lorenzo's right side twirling her long curls in her fingers.

I didn't think much of it until the aroma of Dolce and Gabbana's scent, Light Blue, sparked a memory and I immediately recognized her. The Nivea girl. Although she was still quite attractive, you could tell the years of smoking and anger took their toll on her face. She peered over towards me and ignored the fact that I was there with Lorenzo. She was totally gushing, trying to impress him by making desperate and obvious signs of flipping her hair, licking her glossy lips and tugging on the elastic waistband of her white silk, Valentino jumpsuit to show more cleavage. She kissed his cheek and kept her arm halfway around his right shoulder while trying to touch his neck.

Her bony hips were now leaning into his hip. This was quite intimate for just friends. Hmm, I wondered if his mother put her up to this. The timing was too coincidental, and she was trying way too hard to get his attention. You're a 5'10 glamazon hanging over a fish tank, honey. You got his attention along with everyone else's!

Lorenzo moved backward to put space between their hips and brought me into his left side and said, "Do you remember

Mariella from America from years ago? She is a very successful writer and is back in Italy writing an article."

Nivea girl looked me up and down and said, "Bor-ing."

Her hands slid down Lorenzo's arm and she grabbed his hand saying, "Come out with me Enzo like we used to. I know you miss me. Even your mother said we belong back together."

Lorenzo pulled his hand back and led me toward our table saying to the Nivea girl, "Tell my mother, ciao for me."

She quickly turned her head around in disgust and her Gucci sunglasses fell right off the top of her head into the fish tank! As she tried to catch them, her hands pounded into the water and the water came up and drenched her face and hair. When she brought her hands up, her phone was sopping wet and we could all see her Guccis at the bottom of the fish tank.

Inside, I was dying laughing but kept a straight face so I didn't look as immature as her. Silence can say so much more. I also saw the waiters laughing. No one rushed to offer her a towel because they were all in shock. Lorenzo had the look of "what a pathetic child she is" on his face. I felt so bad…. for the Guccis!

We went to the table and I could hear her huffing and God only knows what she was mumbling. She was literally dripping with desperation. Looking at her brought back memories of Marta. I wasn't sure what to feel and I had so many questions. Why does his mother hate me so much? How does this girl still look so good? What exactly went on between them? Did his mother really send the Nivea girl over here to ruin our night?

Which Nivea products is she using, because I really need them! Would she even tell me? Was this the girl he was engaged to or was she just desperate?

When we sat down, I tried to gauge his emotions but he had a stone face. I've never seen him upset, so I wasn't sure how to proceed.

He looked me straight in the face and said, "You have no worries. I can't stand her and I don't want to be with her. I know she has never been nice to you and she's so jealous of you, even all these years later. The last thing I want is for her to ruin our dinner, our night, or our lives."

Wow, our lives, I thought to myself. "Ok, no worries, let's eat." And that was the last of Nivea girl. For now.

Relief of The Suffering

Suzanne Duchess of St. Alban said this of Padre Pio:

"The fascination of his gruff manner and the magnetism of his extraordinary saintliness drew people to him, and once they had met him, the experience marked them for life."

"Padre Pio had such knowledge of the human soul that Freud could learn from him." Dorothy Valls

The next morning, we headed out early to get as much time as possible in San Giovanni Rotondo. I could tell Lorenzo was nervous. I tried to give him some space while we drove, so there was a lot of silence. Going back there made him feel the same way he did years ago. When I asked him how he felt, he gave the typical female answer of "fine." Oh, hell no, that won't work with me, I thought to myself.

"Lorenzo, what's going on? How are you feeling cause you're acting strange and you're quiet, which never happens?"

He smiled, grabbed my hand and explained to me he was stuck in the feelings of how he felt the last time he was there. He was actually happy and even a little freaked out in a good way that he's going back, especially with me. From the time I sent him the email, he was in awe. He was deeply excited to go back.

When we arrived, we went right to the monastery and his Franciscan friar friends came to greet us. They were completely overjoyed to see him. When they finally got around to noticing me, he introduced me as Mariella from America.

I thought I was going to hear them say "Mamma Mia" out loud, but they stood there with their mouths open.

Enzo laughed and said, "Yes, this is the Mariella from America that I spent so much time crying over. Here she is, back in Italy for a work trip." The priests immediately came over to me and shook my hand as if they were seeing a living miracle and they were.

They asked me if I knew about Padre Pio and I explained to them about the article I'm writing.

"Yes, of course, I know who he is. My parents and grandparents were very devoted to him. They frequently talked about the healings and miracles that God did through him. My mother actually suggested I write about him in my article, so here I am for a quick trip to see San Giovanni Rotondo for myself and to get my miracle."

Lorenzo's priest friend said, "Well, Mariella, you being here is a miracle."

We all laughed, and it was the first time I saw Lorenzo relax that day.

Lorenzo couldn't wait to show me the new church as well as the old church that Padre Pio used to hold mass in when he was alive. Lorenzo spent a lot of time with the friars talking, praying and listening to them give mass. He said it brought him peace to see the millions of pilgrims that go there every year, knowing that their problems were worse than his broken heart. It gave him hope and helped him to use his own sufferings to offer up to God to relieve the suffering of others.

When we arrived at the new church, an overwhelming fragrance that I couldn't put my finger on filled my nose and made me stop in my tracks. I felt like I was walking through someone's perfume cloud, but there was no one at the church and no perfume could linger that long. I have heard about Padre Pio's perfume cloud and most say it smelled like flowers. I can't say it was flowers specifically, but more of a perfume smell. It was light, crisp, and fresh. It reminded me of CK1 by Calvin Klein.

I walked towards the front of the sanctuary and sat in a pew, front and center. I cried. I cried uncontrollably. I cried with gratitude to Padre Pio for bringing me here with the man I love. I thanked my parents, grandparents and great-grandparents for holding onto the tradition of Italy and for teaching me about the miracles of God.

I appreciated growing up knowing how Padre Pio transferred the love and miracles of God to people all over the world to the point that we're still talking about him after his death in 1968. He still appears to people all around the world answering prayers and interceding for us before the throne of God. I'm so grateful and I can't imagine my life without God, Jesus, faith and miracles. I don't necessarily believe in miracles, I depend on them. I also depend on Jesus to get me through the day, sometimes even the minute, especially while driving down the Jersey Turnpike.

My heart was bursting with love for the world. It was one of the times in my life that I felt like God was right there and I could ask him for anything and he would answer. So I asked God to guide me, bring me love and make me an instrument of His love.

Make me a shining bright light of love for the world. Give me strength and guide every step. I sat there crying, praying and holding onto Lorenzo's arm. I knew I could let go with him in the sanctuary. I was grateful for the emotional space. He understood.

After I ran out of tears, we walked around the church and museum. There are so many pictures and beautiful artwork. At the shrine, there was such a heaviness. Everyone was quiet and contemplative.

This is a heavy place for the millions searching for a miracle.

People come here to lay down their heavy burdens. Every chance there was to write a prayer or petition to God around the museum, I did. I wasn't wasting any chances on getting my miracle! I drove too far to not believe with every fiber of my body that God would answer my prayers.

Between the two churches is a beautiful, wide-open space that is the perfect setting for concerts. The set up was already starting for Andrea Bocelli's concert. The original church was beautiful and more traditional, dark and old. It felt so special to walk the same walk and to be in the same space where, not too long ago, Padre Pio also walked. I knew I'd have to come back here. There is too much to write about and so many stories I'd love to hear. No one loves a miracle more than a Catholic Italian. We live for them, literally!

San Giovanni Rotondo is still a little town and I can only imagine how desolate it was before Padre Pio blessed it with his unwavering devotion to God.

The amount of miracles coming from this one man makes you take notice. There is no way thousands and thousands of people all around the world are making up miracles of inexplicable healing, restored relationships, divine guidance and, of course, the stigmata. I was here to get my miracle and to represent the generations of my family that have never been here and will never visit here.

My heart was heavy with their burdens and thinking of them made my throat get tight so that it was noticeable and uncomfortable. I immediately felt guilty for being annoyed by my pain, knowing the pain that Pio went through with the stigmata was nothing in comparison. The weakness of humanity was on full blast in this place that is a spiritual mirror.

We were drained; so we went back to our hotel to relax and talk about our experience. Later on, we ate a simple meal with the Franciscan and Capuchin monks. I always wanted to know if *cappuccino* was really named after them and they told me that *cappuccino* (Italian for "Capuchin") is named after the Capuchin Franciscans. Legend has it that the whipped cream rising to a point reminded some Italians of a Capuchin friar with his long, pointed hood, or *capuche*, and it was dubbed the coffee beverage "*cappuccino.*"

I also asked if they were named after the monkey. They laughed and said it was the other way around. The monkeys reminded the early Spaniards of the friars because their heads appeared shaved like the friars and they seemed to have beards, a trademark of the Capuchins. They called the monkeys *capuchinos,* which has caused the friars a few laughs ever since.

I can see why Enzo loved these monks so much and I only wish Padre Pio was still alive to laugh with us all night.

"Pray, hope and don't worry." – Padre Pio

The next morning, we got another early start and walked around the gardens. It was great exercise going up and down the hills to visit the tourist shops with his priest friends. I had to visit the hospital Padre Pio built. It literally is "hope on a hill." It's magnificent, majestic and splendid. What an accomplishment and what a way to show your love for the world.

It's a perfect example of what one person can do when God is at the helm. The hospital, *Casa Sollievo della Sofferenza*, [Home for Relief of the Suffering] opened May 5, 1956. I love the name, and this is what a hospital should be called. Everyone should remember that is the true purpose of a hospital, just like the church.

I wanted to buy everything in the gift shops around town and then I realized I'd have a Padre Pio shrine in my house which might look crazy. I agreed to wait to build my shrine after I get my miracle! I made sure to get my mother her magnet for the fridge that she made me promise to get for her. I'd never hear the end of it if I went to Padre Pio's town and didn't bring home a magnet!

I was so excited to hear Bocelli sing at the shrine today. Knowing that he also loves Padre Pio made it seem as if he was carrying the torch from Beniamino Gigli, to the future generations.

When he started singing *Mamma*, the crowd roared. It was so special, and we all started singing as if we were singing it for and to Pio. The Holy Spirit was there for sure and no doubt Padre Pio was as well. He would never miss this song.

Friar Ermelindo described Gigli as "one of the best singers of that time" and "a good friend of Padre Pio. Padre Pio also asked him to sing the song *Mama*, because Padre Pio was very fond of his mama," Fr. Ermelindo said, Padre Pio loved music and Fr. Ermelindo also said that he saw many singers come to visit Padre Pio. Gigli was devoted to the beautiful, sacred music of Don Lorenzo Perosi, from whom he drew much of his inspiration. There is a reason why sacred songs have lasted the test of time and have universal appeal.

The beauty of the concert, scenery and the people glowing with joy made me feel that being here with Lorenzo and seeing Bocelli sing is my miracle. I'm totally satisfied if this is my miracle because it sure feels like one to me.

Before leaving the shrine, we returned to the new church to see if we could still smell the fragrance in the air again. We did! It was so intoxicating.

I was emotionally drained from praying so hard, looking for wisdom and direction, so this brought me back to life. It was as if I emptied my spirit the first time I entered the church and then refilled before I left. My work there was done. Let's eat!

We went back to our hotel for a drink at the bar and a nap. When I woke up from my nap, there was a beautifully wrapped box next to me where Lorenzo once slept. Next to the present sat Lorenzo, with a chilled glass of Prosecco and the biggest smile on his face. I totally forgot about the present he bought for me at Cinque's store. I was so excited and so was he. I quickly sat up to untie the ribbon, but he grabbed my hand to stop me.

Enzo looked up at me and said, "Mariella, *ti amo* [I love you] and I want to spend the rest-a my life with you."

I started to respond, and he put his hand over my mouth to stop me from speaking.

He continued, "I never want us to be apart again and I will do whatever it takes to be with you. I will move to America or you to Italia."

My heart was beating out of my chest.

"I hope you feel-a the same. Open the box."

Those green eyes pierced my soul. All I could do was smile. I was frozen.

I took a deep breath and untied Cinque's perfectly tied ribbon and when I removed the top, there was the most beautiful rose gold colored, satin baby-doll dress with taffeta underneath. The trim was beads, and sequin for a beautiful subtle sparkle. It was exquisite. When I lifted the dress out of the box, a small velvet pouch dropped into my lap. I figured it was extra sequins and beads that often come with beaded dresses.

Lorenzo took the bag, opened it, and got down on one knee. He pulled out the most exquisite rose gold and pink diamond ring from the bag. He asked me to marry him and promised to figure it all out, no matter what happens.

Dress, what dress? I burst into tears with love, excitement and all the emotions that I've been denying for years. I threw my arms around him and said, "YES, yes, yes, of course."

"To think I was so happy with only a dress." I said. We laughed and clinked our glasses and giggled like school kids. I don't remember giggling like this with him. It was like he was finally able to relax and let go. All I could do was look at this gorgeous ring. Thank God he has exquisite taste.

"Oh, Lorenzo, does your mother know?" I had to ask him.

"Yes, she knows, and she approves," he said with a smile.

I couldn't think of all the real details and logistics of how this could work. I knew I wanted it to work out so badly and I was willing to do anything possible to make it work. Anything. We sat in the bed hugging each other and laughing. I always imagined how my wedding proposal would happen, but this was so much better and so unexpected.

We showered together and had our first engaged couple lovemaking session. It was different. I can't explain it, but it was like this time was for real and all the other times were for fun. Not that we didn't have fun, but this added a whole other level of connection. It was deep and loving and I've never felt so close to anyone in my life. It was like we were finally one.

I was his, and he was mine. Before we turned into raisins, we had to get out of the shower. After finishing my hair and makeup, I put on my new dress and did a little twirl for Lorenzo. I asked if he liked my engagement dress.

"I like it so-a much, I want to rip if off-a you right now."

"No, Lorenzo, I just got pretty." I laughingly said.

"Already, you are-a telling me no to sex? It has only been an hour and now I can't have you again?" he said with those puppy dog eyes.

"Lorenzo, I want to eat and build up energy, so when we return, we can finish what we started. Don't worry, this shower was the appetizer and I will be your dessert." I said with a sexy smile and hopped on his lap.

"Mmmmm, mamma mia, I want dessert first." he moaned. He grabbed my butt cheeks, pushed me into his hips and stood up while holding me. "I am going to carry you all over Italy like this and never let you go." We laughed, hugged, and left to eat.

I felt like such a princess; A real life princess. I had a gorgeous, sparkling diamond, a beautiful, sparkling dress and a prince with beautiful sparkling eyes. I got another dose of Italian magic and my miracle. I couldn't wait to tell everyone. My mother will freak out but I wanted this to be our special night. I'll call her tomorrow. All I could think about was how special this was happening in San Giovanni Rotondo with pictures of Padre Pio all over the town looking down upon us and blessing our future marriage.

As we passed a picture of Padre Pio in a store window, Enzo stopped and put his forehead on the glass and mumbled something in Italian and then said, "Grazie, Padre Pio." Then he rested his head there for a minute. When he turned his head to look at me, he had a distinct look on his face. It was a look of being very calm, pensive, satisfied.

He grabbed my hand, pulled me into his chest, put his arm around me and guided me as I walked on the cobblestone in my heels with my new princess dress.

I was so excited about dinner because I've never been to the East Coast of Italy. The food did not disappoint. We went to a restaurant called Opus Wine, tucked away in a corner down a cobblestone street that no one could drive through unless they were Italian! We started with a 2014 red wine called Marramiero Inferi. I just about died. It was so good. It felt like the owner's recommendation was such that he knew my soul. We ate the most amazing piece of beef and Lorenzo told me that southeastern Italy is popular for meat. I've had some good meat in my life, but this might be the best I've ever had. We shared pistachio and shrimp with *paccheri* [pasta shape] and *burrata* [cheese]. Then we had veal with dried tomatoes and capers.

I'll eat almost anything with capers because it reminds me of my grandmother's Christmas Eve *aglio oglio* [garlic, oil], and anchovy spaghetti dish. The restaurant has a casual atmosphere that feels like you're in a library but instead of books it was bottles of wine on the shelves. The food was pure art and elegance. I feel like this whole town is blessed and the people are wonderful. I never thought I could live anywhere in Italy except for Sorrento, but I could live here!

After dinner, we walked around the piazza. Everyone was out looking their best. All the young single people were in their groups checking out the opposite sex and trying to flirt. It brought back such memories. Suddenly, we heard a very familiar beat. We walked closer to the center of the town square to hear the song. It was a club remix of *We Speak No Americano*. I knew this version because it was sung by a very popular, Italian-American, Jersey boy named Giorgio.

I looked at Enzo and said, "Remember when that was us?"

He laughed and said, "Yes, and here I am-a, still singing to my Americana."

We laughed, and he took my hand to twirl me in synch with the music. We came across a café and got some espresso before going back to the hotel. As we squeezed up to the counter to order, it suddenly hit me. I looked at Lorenzo and asked, "Lorenzo, did you have that ring in the dress box the whole time from Positano to tonight?"

A look of pure guilt came over his face, then a look of pure joy over pulling it off and totally surprising me.

"Yes, I surprise-a you, yes?"

"Yes, totally. I had no idea, and you never slipped or gave me any hint at all."

I couldn't believe he never once gave it away or acted weird. He was totally cool, confident, and secure. I was so excited about all the rest of the surprises he had planned for us. He was always full of surprises. I don't know why I thought this would be any different. It was as much fun for him to think of these things as it was for me to receive them. I was definitely not as creative.

Before entering our hotel room, he swept me off my feet and carried me over the threshold. It was almost impossible to keep our hands off of each other. There was no doubt for either of us. I'd marry him right now, if I could. In a matter of seconds, he threw me over his shoulders, smacked my butt and then bit it so hard, I screamed. He felt bad, so he covered my butt in kisses and many, *mi dispiace*.

He sat me on the counter in the bathroom, turned on the faucet and dripped some freezing cold water down my cleavage, followed by his warm tongue. He was very aware of carefully removing the dress. I'm sure he remembered how expensive it was because he was not usually too careful when ripping my clothes off. I wrapped my legs around him and pushed him into me so hard that even he moaned. I couldn't get enough of him. I didn't want one inch of my body to not be touching his. Needless to say, we finished what we started before dinner and what could be better than having dessert and burning calories at the same time?

The next morning, we had a very early breakfast with the friars to show them my ring and made one last visit to the new and old shrine. I had to experience that air again and give thanks. Being there made me feel like I was looking into a mirror but I saw my soul instead of my face. It was a very bittersweet goodbye to Padre Pio and the friars. We all cried tears of joy. They made me feel so welcome since they knew our entire story. I was like a walking miracle; now with a big diamond!

While Enzo was hugging the friars goodbye, he started crying in the friar's arms. He was so happy and grateful that he could bring me there to show them their prayers were answered in so many ways. So much gratitude and joy filled our hearts.

We let out years of waiting for God to answer our prayers. We promised to get back there sooner rather than later, and it was not an empty promise. When we got in the car, Lorenzo was quiet for a long time. I felt God had his hand over my mouth, making sure I gave him his space to think, feel, and decompress.

Our Lady of the Rosary

"The Rosary is the weapon for these times." Padre Pio

About two hours into our trip, I asked him if we could go to Our Lady of the Rosary Shrine in Pompeii. The same church I went to and asked Mary to make Lorenzo my husband. Lorenzo was happy to go, and when we got there, I couldn't wait to get inside and give thanks to God. He asked why I was so excited to go there, so I told him what happened when I went there years ago and what I asked Mary to do for me. I wasn't sure he believed me.

As we walked up to the painting named, *Our Lady of the Rosary*, I pulled out the rosary that Lorenzo gave me years ago when I was leaving Massa. He was shocked to see it and I think that actually made him believe what I was saying. I told him I have been waiting and dreaming of coming here with him and this rosary. The priceless artwork of Mother Mary and young Jesus presenting the rosary to Saint Dominic and Saint Catherine of Siena was more beautiful than I remembered. We held hands with the rosary woven between our fingers and it really was the tie that bound us together, then; now, and in the future.

We said some prayers, and a joyful mystery from the rosary. We lit some candles, took some pictures and continued to the airport.

In the car, it hit me like a ton of bricks.

"Oh no, Lorenzo, I totally forgot to call my mother. She's gonna freak out."

He looked at me and said, "Call my mother-in-law. My new mamma. I wanna talk to her!"

I dug into my purse for my phone, punched in mother's name and when she answered, I said, "Maaa, you're never gonna believe what happened."

La Fine - The End

To read what happens next with Mariella and Lorenzo, be sure to pick up Lora's next book, The Prosecco Princess.

More Food, Romance And Travels Coming Your Way!

www.thebeautybuster.com

About The Author

Lora Condon is an international award-winning esthetician and a New York Times featured writer. Her no-holds bared, Jersey girl attitude has made her a favorite with beauty editors, magazines and even some TV shows. *Spa Wars–The Ugly Truth About the Beauty Industry*, her first book, was featured in the *New York Times*, *American Spa Magazine* and *Dr. Oz*.

Dermascope Magazine's, Favorite Contributing Writer of 2020 has also contributed to many magazines, blogs and tv shows. Her appearances on *Dr. Oz*, *Entertainment Tonight* and Brazilian National TV have catapulted her to the top of the beauty industry with InStyle Magazine considering her the Best Brow Shaper in NJ.

Her work has been seen in Oprah Magazine, Good Morning America, Fox News, CNN, The View, Olive Garden, Burger King, Fresh, Party Monster, Page 6 of the NY Post, and NY Daily News.

She has created content to help develop multi-million dollar brands within the beauty industry over the last 20 years. She still loves to help brands grow their uniqueness.

Her love for Italy and high-quality skin products led her to create a skin line using the purest of olive oils from her family's town of Postiglione, Italy. Yes, the town featured in this book. You can purchase these products at www.thebeautybuster.com

The closest wine Lora can get that tastes like the wine she gets in Italy sells through her Scout & Cellar website. **Email Lora for wine recommendations here at www.scoutandcellar.com/yourwinegirl or watch her wine videos on YouTube.**

Stay tuned for the continuation of *Love on the Amalfi Coast* with the forthcoming book, *The Prosecco Princess.*

To keep up with everything Lora is doing, visit her site www.thebeautybuster.com

Facebook – International Love On The Amalfi Coast or The Beauty Buster for beauty related updates

Instgram - Love On The Amalfi Coast

Printed in Great Britain
by Amazon